BROTHERS OF LIGHT
The Penitentes of the Southwest

BROTHERS OF LIGHT

The Penitentes of the Southwest
by
Alice Corbin Henderson

Illustrations by William Penhallow Henderson

Introduction to this Edition by Lynn Cline

SANTA FE

New Material © 2013 by Sunstone Press. All Rights Reserved.

No part of this book may be reproduced in any form or by any electronic or mechanical means including information storage and retrieval systems without permission in writing from the publisher, except by a reviewer who may quote brief passages in a review.

Sunstone books may be purchased for educational, business, or sales promotional use. For information please write: Special Markets Department, Sunstone Press, P.O. Box 2321, Santa Fe, New Mexico 87504-2321.

Library of Congress Cataloging-in-Publication Data

Henderson, Alice Corbin, 1881-1949.
  Brothers of light : the Penitentes of the Southwest / by Alice Corbin Henderson ; illustrations by William Penhallow Henderson ; introduction to this edition by Lynn Cline.
    pages cm. -- (Southwest heritage series)
  Originally published: New York : Harcourt, Brace, 1937.
  ISBN 978-0-86534-894-3 (pbk. : alk. paper)
  1. Hermanos Penitentes. I. Title.
  BX3653.U6H3 2012
  267'.242789--dc23
                        2012048624

WWW.SUNSTONEPRESS.COM
SUNSTONE PRESS / POST OFFICE BOX 2321 / SANTA FE, NM 87504-2321 /USA
(505) 988-4418 / ORDERS ONLY (800) 243-5644 / FAX (505) 988-1025

CONTENTS

I / THE SOUTHWEST HERITAGE SERIES / vii

II / INTRODUCTION TO THIS EDITION / ix

III / A REVIEW / xv
The New Mexico Quarterly, 1937

IV / THE HENDERSONS: PIONEERS OF
ORIGINAL ART COLONY / xvii
The Santa Fe New Mexican, 2011

V / ALICE CORBIN, AN APPRECIATION / xxi
New Mexico Quarterly Review, 1949

VI / BROTHERS OF LIGHT / lxi
1937 EDITION

SOUTHWEST HERITAGE SERIES

I

THE SOUTHWEST HERITAGE SERIES

"The past is not dead. In fact, it's not even past."
—William Faulkner, *Requiem for a Nun*

The history of the United States is written in hundreds of regional histories and literary works. Those letters, essays, memoirs, biographies and even collections of fiction are often first-hand accounts by people who wanted to memorialize an event, a person or simply record for posterity the concerns and issues of the times. Many of these accounts have been lost, destroyed or overlooked. Some are in private or public collections but deemed to be in too fragile condition to permit handling by contemporary readers and researchers.

However, now with the application of twenty-first century technology, nineteenth and twentieth century material can be reprinted and made accessible to the general public. These early writings are the DNA of our history and culture and are essential to understanding the present in terms of the past.

The Southwest Heritage Series is a form of literary preservation. Heritage by definition implies legacy and these early works are our legacy from those who have gone before us. To properly present and preserve that legacy, no changes in style or contents have been made. The material reprinted stands on its own as it first appeared. The point of view is that of the author and the era in which he or she lived. We would not expect photographs of people from the past to be re-imaged with modern clothes, hair styles and backgrounds. We should not, therefore, expect their ideas and personal philosophies to reflect our modern concepts.

Remember, reading their words and sharing their thoughts is a passport back into understanding how the past was shaped and how it influenced today's world.

Our hope is that new access to these older books will provide readers with a challenging and exciting experience.

II

INTRODUCTION TO THIS EDITION
by
Lynn Cline

Without Alice Corbin Henderson, Santa Fe, New Mexico, might never have become a celebrated sanctuary and inspirational touchstone for artists, writers and other creative souls who have made their homes here for the past two centuries.

Alice was a wife, mother and also the first associate editor of *Poetry*, an influential magazine published out of Chicago, when she first sojourned to the Southwest seeking a cure for a serious case of tuberculosis.

Traveling by train from her home in Chicago with her husband, William Penhallow Henderson, and young daughter, Little Alice, she arrived in 1916, fully expecting to die within a year. She never could have predicted how life in Santa Fe would fully transform her.

Initially staying at the famous Sunmount Sanatorium and then moving into a house her husband built on Camino Monte Sol, she tapped into a deep and profound well of creativity. As a result, she survived her bout with tuberculosis, living on for years and producing a steady stream of acclaimed poetry, prose, essays and a prized book, the *WPA Guide to New Mexico*, published in 1940.

Alice Corbin Henderson became the first and founding member of the Santa Fe writers' colony. By the time she arrived at Sunmount Sanatorium, she already had established herself as a prominent editor in America's poetry scene. She also had written two books of poetry, by the time tuberculosis threatened to destroy everything she had accomplished. Informing her that she would not live for more than a year, her doctor prescribed a stay at Sunmount.

Traveling to New Mexico by train in March 1916, Henderson must have been terrified facing certain death. Later, she recorded what was running through her mind as she voyaged into an unknown country:

"I had been thrown out into the desert to die, like a piece of old scrap-iron, or a rusty Ford." Yet, instead of death, she discovered a whole new way of life.

In a letter sent to poet Carl Sandburg on March 28, she described the vistas from Sunmount cottage that took in the "sand-combed valley to the west," the "mesas rising out of it" and the "snow-capped mountains of the Sangre de Cristo range."

Sandburg's return letter of April 2nd delivered an eloquent description of how New Mexico had transformed Henderson: she had "slipped into quiet, pearl-walled caves of quiet, and was learning new values of dream," he wrote to her. Sandburg, the recipient of two Pulitzer prizes, visited Santa Fe in the 1920s and 1930s, serenading guests with folk songs as he played guitar at a reception Henderson held in his honor.

Henderson's own writing reflected her transformation. The place she had once believed would be a "desolate exile," instead astounded her as "a new world of beauty."

Alice Corbin Henderson left Sunmount after her recovery and, from 1917 to 1923, lived in a small adobe house on what was then called Telegraph Road. (In keeping with her desire to celebrate traditional culture, Henderson convinced city authorities to officially change Telegraph Road's name back to its original Spanish name, Camino del Monte Sol, or Road of the Sun Mountain, which it bears today.)

In 1924, Henderson's husband built the family a larger home nearby, in the same area where other artists who recently settled in Santa Fe built their homes and studios. William Penhallow Henderson, an acclaimed architect of Santa Fe Style, also designed an elegant adobe on Garcia Street which now houses the School of American Research as well as the Wheelwright Museum building on Museum Hill.

The Henderson home became a meeting place for the growing group of writers, artists, and intellectuals who settled in Santa Fe. Here, Henderson came to know a different rhythm and way of life, living a slower pace than Chicago offered that connected her to the cycles of the seasons. Restored to good health, Henderson experimented with a new style of writing, one that celebrated the simplicity of life in northern New Mexico.

In 1920, Henderson published her acclaimed *Red Earth: Poems of*

New Mexico, which included work first published in *Poetry* magazine. In American Modernist scholar Lois Palken Rudnick's introduction to the 2003 reissue of *Red Earth*, she wrote that Henderson's book instantly took an important place in modern American poetry "both because of its aesthetic power and because the poems selected for it made an important contribution to the culture wars that were occurring over the formation of the modern poetry canon in the early twentieth century."

The untitled poem below, which Henderson placed at the beginning of *Red Earth*, signaled to readers that they were embarking on a voyage to an unfamiliar and powerful land full of vast open space and silences—a remote place in the country that greatly contrasted the bustling, noisy and busy pace of life in the city:

> After the roar, after the fierce modern music
> Of rivets and hammers and trams,
> After the shout of the giant,
> Youthful and brawling and strong
> Building the cities of men,
> Here is the desert of silence,
> Blinking and blind in the sun—
> An old, old woman who mumbles her beads
> And crumbles to stone.

Henderson also promoted New Mexico in numerous other ways, compiling the 1928 groundbreaking book, *The Turquoise Trail, An Anthology of New Mexico Poetry*, containing work by 37 contributors, all of whom who drew inspiration from New Mexico. In her preface to the anthology, Henderson described similarities between New Mexico's diverse cultures:

> "On the common ground of poetry, indeed, the living Indian poets and the Anglo-American poets of New Mexico now meet in friendly contact; and the influence of this primitive verse and thought on the later poets is obvious."

Henderson joined Santa Fe writer Raymond Otis and poets

Haniel Long and Peggy Pond Church as a founding member of Writers' Editions, a cooperative publishing venture of Santa Fe and Taos writers launched in the mid-1930s.

The highly successful group, known as Rydal Press, had its own printer's mark—a small saint cradling two printer's inking balls between his hands—drafted by illustrator and type inventor Warren Chappell. Rydal Press was the moniker chosen by Walter Lippincott Goodwin, Jr., a talented printer and publisher from Pennsylvania invited to Santa Fe by Writers' Editions in 1933.

The Writers' Editions' credo, which appeared on most of its books, mandated that regional publication must "foster the growth of American literature." The group's 17 publications reflected the varied voices of the region. Writers' Editions published three poetry books, including Alice Corbin Henderson's *The Sun Turns West*, containing work from 1915 to 1932.

Alice Corbin Henderson kept busy with other projects too. Her passion for eclectic songs resulted in *Brothers of the Light: The Penitentes of the Southwest*, a collection of Spanish religious songs sung by the Penitentes, a secretive group of Hispano Catholic men. Published in 1937 with illustrations by Henderson's husband, the book also contained information about the group's history and ritual ceremonies.

Henderson also contributed to *New Mexico: A Guide to the Colorful State*, one of a series of travel guides to American states launched by the Works Progress Administration to increase tourism during the Depression years.

Because of its scope, the book took longer to complete than planned and when it finally was published in 1940, it contained Henderson's informative essay on New Mexico literature. The essay opens with the acknowledgement that New Mexico's literary tradition "begins with orally transmitted myths, legends and rituals of the Indians who were native to the soil when the Spaniards came," and that the first written books were "the old Spanish chronicles of exploration and conquest."

Undoubtedly, Alice Corbin Henderson was one of the main movers and shakers of the Santa Fe writers' colony. She also had strong ties to the Taos literary colony: at age 15 her daughter, known as Little Alice, married Mabel Dodge Luhan's only son, John Evans. The marriage didn't last, but the couple did have daughters before they divorced in 1932.

It's difficult to know whether Alice Corbin Henderson was pleased by the marriage. After all, she and Mabel Dodge Luhan were not the best of friends. Indeed, Alice may be the main reason why Mabel chose to settle in Taos rather than Santa Fe. Since Alice was already happily ensconced in Santa Fe when Mabel arrived in 1917, Mabel fled to Taos, almost certainly because she did not intend to take on a rival in her search to become the pivotal force in whatever town she inhabited.

And while Mabel was prolific, penning a series of autobiographies in at least five volumes as well as dozens of articles published in national magazines, newspapers and other periodicals, Alice Corbin Henderson was by far the better writer.

Alice not only wrote and edited in Santa Fe, she had an impressively busy social life, hosting literary readings, teas, grand balls and launching the annual Writer's Round-Up, a huge gala attended by just about every writer and artist in town.

Alice's role in the Santa Fe writers' colony was major. When artists, authors and other creatives began to trek to northern New Mexico in the early twentieth century, fleeing a modern world obsessed with war, greed, and excessive materialism, Alice became their guide. She introduced writers and artists to poets that she had discovered and nurtured in the pages of *Poetry*, including Ezra Pound, Carl Sandburg and Vachel Lindsay. And when Robert Frost came to town, it was because Alice had invited him.

These writers took solace in the different cultures and rhythms of the Southwest, treasuring their experiences of the ancient traditions of the Pueblo, Navajo and Hopi people and the Hispano people who set roots in New Mexico starting in the 16th century.

These prolific pilgrims of the 20th century firmly believed that life in a remote and foreign land offered an antidote to urbanization, industrialization, and a sickly preoccupation with military power that overtook America starting with World War I.

Northern New Mexico's dry desert air, forested mountains, flat-top mesas, and sun-drenched sky have always wielded a rough sort of magic on its denizens, but this lively group of writers who established literary colonies in Santa Fe and Taos from the early 1900s took the effects to new heights.

They arrived on the heels of a group of national and international artists, who had founded their colonies in Santa Fe and Taos a few years earlier. The group, which also included architects, anthropologists and history buffs frequently collaborated on projects as well as personal achievements, creating books, magazine articles, and group exhibitions along with marriages, families and friendships.

These celebrated intellectuals—including British author D.H. Lawrence, American author Willa Cather, American poet and naturalist Mary Austin and American poet Witter Bynner—saw no place for themselves or their work in urban centers and industrialized societies.

Henderson was a well-liked, gifted writer who had more impact probably than any other writer of her era in Santa Fe. Her husband died of a heart attack in 1943, but she—who had been told she would die within a year in 1916—lived a full life until July 18, 1949. A few months before her death, Henderson's friends and colleagues paid tribute to her invaluable role as a poet, editor, and activist in Santa Fe with a special edition of *New Mexico Quarterly Review*, published by the University of New Mexico.

Edited by Santa Fe poet Witter Bynner and Santa Fe author Oliver La Farge, the commemorative edition contained glowing accounts of her friendship and professional stature in the community and is included in this book from Sunstone Press.

Bynner may have put it best, in his essay, "Alice and I," when he wrote that during "that golden period of American poetry, her vivid, sympathetic spirit meant much more to most of the poets who made it golden, as it has meant much to all of us who have encountered her in poetry or in life."

III

A REVIEW
The New Mexico Quarterly
May 1937, Vol. VII, Number 2, Page 149
by
T. M. Pearce

There is no single topic which has been more exploited to make drama of this ancient state of New Mexico than Los Hermanos Penitentes. From the earliest accounts of nineteenth century Americanos down to the last Associated Press dispatch in Holy Week, the pageant of flagellation and the mimetic suffering of the Christ-path to Calvary has been surrounded with all that is thrill conveying and blood chilling. It is a sure theme to arrest the attention of a recent visitor or to center the interest of a gathering away from New Mexico. Yet very little of the real life of the Penitentes has been revealed by these news items or by the casual inspection of the rites.

Mrs. Alice Henderson's book is a friendly and picturing account of the Brothers of Light. She has not written to make melodrama of them nor to psychoanalyze. Her intention is to present the folk-way of this very real experience by a vivid picture of it plus conclusions as to the European background and references to the developments of the cult in New Mexico. This she has done as only one living in New Mexico for many years can do—with respect and liking for the New Mexican scene and the life related to it.

Imagine as amphitheater a stretch of sun-bleached soil extending from the valley of the Rio Grande to the foothills of the Sangre de Cristo mountains. The river itself is hidden by leafless, silvery-white cottonwoods, and from these the eye ranges across sandy hillocks up to a ridge of red cliffs cutting against blue snow-capped mountains. Over all is the bright clear light of an early spring day; and certainly nothing could be more open and free and remote from mystery than this level stretch of country bared to the candid light of the steady mountain sun.

So the writer sets the stage for the strange, unearthly procession which winds up the sandy ridge in the raw wintry air, the *pitero* sounding thin reedy notes while black-veiled figures stagger under heavy crosses, and other men, bared to the waist, lift the yucca lashes at rhythmic intervals to come down across their flesh with a stinging thud. We go with the author to the morado and the ceremony of the *tinieblas*, the darkness and the rent veil of the temple during the hours of Calvary. We meet the Hermano Mayor at Abiqui. We learn of the fraternal and charitable services of the organization, and we learn that it is strongly inwrought in the life of the laity in the isolated parishes of New Mexico where the ministrations of priest or friar have never been as consistently performed as those of the brotherhood.

The author has not sentimentalized her report. She does not pretend to be or to have been a part of this fellowship. Yet insofar as one not a Penitente can record the rites, Mrs. Henderson has succeeded and with appropriate deference to the initiates. William Penhallow Henderson is fellow to this interpretation with some unusual drawings in black and white which catch the play of the light in scenes of dusk and day as light is always a factor of emphasis in this State which belongs to the Sun.

IV

THE HENDERSONS: PIONEERS OF ORIGINAL ART COLONY
by
Marc Simmons
The Santa Fe New Mexican, February 25, 2011

A while ago I saw a beautiful three-page advertisement offering for sale the Tesuque estate of William Penhallow Henderson, one of the pioneer founders of the original Santa Fe art colony. I assumed the impressive Santa Fe-style mansion pictured was "El Cuervo" (The Raven) that Henderson had designed for his daughter and her husband in the mid-1920s.

A nationally known portrait painter, muralist and architect, he had come to Santa Fe from Chicago with wife Alice Corbin Henderson in 1916. She was suffering from tuberculosis and entered the Sunmount Sanatorium on the eastern edge of the capital city. For several years, Alice had served as associate editor of the magazine *Poetry*, rubbing shoulders with the likes of Carl Sandburg, Ezra Pound and Robert Frost. As her health improved at Sunmount, she began falling under New Mexico's spell, and in time would become one of its chief promoters.

The Hendersons had arrived on the scene just as local civic organizations were joining forces to transform Santa Fe into a tourist mecca. They touted the city's cultural attractions, its history, archaeology, adobe architecture and sang the praises of the landscape's "addictive qualities." The boosters, taking note of Taos' success in attracting artists, saw the potential profits in following that example. History would prove them right, for by the end of the century, Santa Fe's art market had become one of the mainstays of its economy.

William and Alice were among the vanguard of newcomers in the arts who managed to lure former friends and associates from the East to pay Santa Fe a visit. Some of those liked what they found and stayed.

When Alice's health improved, she left the sanatorium and with her family moved into a small adobe house on Telephone Road, so named because the phone line followed it to the city center. Shortly, she persuaded local officials to rename it Camino del Monte Sol. A few years later, William saw to the building of a more spacious family home down the same street. By that time, the Camino, as it was generally known, had become the residence of a handful of writers and artists and the focal point of the colony.

The Hendersons led the way in introducing later arrivals to "the glories" of accessible Indian and Hispano cultures. After her visits into the countryside, Alice wrote descriptive poems of Pueblo dances. And in 1937, she published a book, *Brothers of Light, The Penitentes of the Southwest*, with illustrations by her husband. It was an early sympathetic treatment of this secretive Hispanic religious brotherhood.

Alice Corbin Henderson's most substantial work was her 1928 volume, *The Turquoise Trail, An Anthology of New Mexico Poetry*, which she edited herself. It contained poems from 37 contributors, including such luminaries as Mary Austin, D.H. Lawrence, Peggy Pond Church, Paul Horgan, Willa Cather and, of course, Alice herself.

William, for his part, was painting away in his studio and producing a series of historical murals in the U.S. Courthouse on South Federal Place. But he also plied his trade as a part-time architect and builder. To do that, he opened his own construction company, which, in 1937, designed and built the Museum of Navajo Ceremonial Art (known today as the Wheelwright Museum of the American Indian), among other structures. Alice put on another of her many hats and became its first curator and librarian.

As they aged, the Hendersons went to live with their daughter in El Cuervo. After nine tranquil years there, William Penhallow Henderson in 1943 died of a sudden heart attack at age 66. Alice, grieving, continued to write poems and engage in projects dedicated to preserving New Mexico's cultural traditions until her death in 1949.

Sadly, in spite of the major role the Hendersons played in launching Santa Fe's artist and writer colonies, memory of their part has faded in recent years. Sale of the Tesuque estate reminded me of that.

Alice Corbin Henderson and William Penhallow Henderson, 1932.
Photograph by Will Connell. Courtesy Palace of the Governors Photo Archives
(NMHM/DCA, Negative Number 059757).

V

ALICE CORBIN, AN APPRECIATION
edited by
Witter Bynner and Oliver La Farge
New Mexico Quarterly Review
Spring, 1949
Volume XIX, No. 1

Alice Corbin Henderson, born in St. Louis, Missouri, married to William Penhallow Henderson, the artist, in 1905, and mother of one daughter, Mrs. Edgar L. Rossin, published her first book, *Adam's Dream, and Two Other Miracle Plays for Children*, in 1907, and the second, *The Spinning Woman of the Sky*, a volume of poems, in 1912. At this time she also became active in the literary world as fellow-founder and associate editor with Harriet Monroe of *Poetry: a Magazine of Verse*. In her editorial post, which she held until 1916, she was largely instrumental in the discovery and encouragement of Midwestern and other verse since become famous. She compiled with Harriet Monroe *The New Poetry*, an anthology published in 1917. Not only poets who were then local, like Carl Sandburg, Edgar Lee Masters, and Vachel Lindsay, owe much to her ardent interest; a poet as remote from these others as Ezra Pound, iconoclast and expatriate, has given frequent testimony of debt to her.

After her resignation from editorial work and her move to New Mexico because of ill health, she published two books of verse, *Red Earth* in 1920, and *The Sun Turns West* in 1933, during which time she also compiled an anthology of New Mexico Poetry, *The Turquoise Trail*, published in 1928. *Brothers of Light, the Penitentes of the Southwest*, her first book of prose, an authentic and notable contribution to both history and literature, was published in 1937.

Mrs. Henderson is now living at Tesuque, New Mexico, near Santa Fe, where for over thirty years she has been a vital and loved leader in the community and a constant espouser of good causes.

ALICE AND I
Witter Bynner

In tireder or wiser age one abstains both from giving and from attending lectures. In my comparative youth, the date being 1921, I arrived in Santa Fe to give one. The town was off my professional beat; but I had asked a reluctant agent to swing me here, unprofitably, between Oklahoma and Colorado and to let me have a week's respite besides. Because of influenza, in one of those years when influenza was not just a cold, I took more than the week's respite, had to stay in Santa Fe six weeks to recover and have been recuperating here ever since. The person who was to blame for all this is Alice Corbin.

In an earlier year of lecturing—1916 I think—I had been heckled from the floor at Chicago. My subject was "Contemporary American Poetry"; and, before the secret had broken that Arthur Davison Ficke and I were respectively Anne Knish and Emanuel Morgan, founders and wielders of the Spectric School of Poetry, I was telling my audience how superior Spectric verse was to Imagist verse. I was advancing the Spectric theory. The poet is imbued with a subject or faces one suddenly. Instead of emotionalizing or intellectualizing his approach to it, he blanks his conscious heart, his deliberate mind, and lets the subject submerge him both from inside and from outside. He acts as a medium and records the force and range of his theme in a mode seemingly beyond his control. It might have been called the Ouija School of Poetry; but on a brash platform I was taking our "school" more solemnly than my conscience should have permitted. I was preferring the specter to the image and probably confusing image with imagery, when an interruption came from the audience. A woman's voice gave us the Imagists' insistence that an image was not a mere figure of speech but a clearly seen picture of an idea. In a sharp but friendly interchange between auditor and lecturer, was the former unwittingly siding with earlier artists who would nowadays be called representational, and the latter unwittingly siding with present-day artists who believe the inner consciousness chooses better pictures than the outer consciousness? Brittle though our talk was, each of us was thinking he had the better of the tilt, a liking sparked between us; and after the lecture Alice Corbin and I shook hands and planned to join again. We did join shortly afterwards at the Hendersons' studio in Chicago, where I met Alice's painter-husband, William Penhallow Henderson, and their diminutive daughter.

I was wandering in those days, still young, still lecturing, the commercialized troubadour, and from time to time I saw the Hendersons in Chicago. Some years later I heard that Alice was ill, that she was in Santa Fe for her health, and I wrote her. In answering she proposed that I come to Santa Fe on one of my tours. And so I came.

It had not occurred to me that she was seriously ill. I had thought merely that Santa Fe was a better climate for her. And so, when I stepped off the primitive car which a spur track brought from Lamy into a town of nine thousand, I thought I was greeting with a kiss the Alice I had sparred with in Chicago and thought I was giving my luggage to a broad-hatted cowboy hand from some frontier hotel. Not until we had almost reached the sanitarium did I realize that the Alice alongside me was the diminutive daughter, now grown to fifteen, that the cowboy-hand in the front seat with my luggage, who had not till now said a word, was William Penhallow Henderson and that the elder Alice was a bedded invalid.

Though it troubled me at first to stay in a building which was half hotel, half sanitarium for tuberculars, I was soon persuaded that I was safer at Sunmount than in a New York trolley car and I remained beyond the six weeks needed for recovery from influenza. Alice Corbin's room, perhaps purposely, was opposite the doctor's office. She was not only a bed-patient but under strict watch as to rest and diet. Doctors, nurses, servants, and patients were all, in those years, easy comrades and so were such guests as lived long enough in the haphazard hotel section to become fellow Santa Feans. Waitresses would bring coffee for groups in this or that private room instead of serving it at this or that table in the long dining hall. Later Alice brewed her own coffee, and we would gather nightly in her room for gay, swift talk and forbidden cigarettes. Now and then we would enjoy in our coffee cups a fill or two of Taos Lightning, that fiery corn whiskey which we keg-rolled in the backs of our cars. Willy would be there, Little Alice would be there, a nurse would be there. Finally even the head doctor would be there and almost grant that these trespasses upon rule were doing his patient good.

In spite or because of such trespass, Alice presently emerged from the sanitarium, well enough to move to the little house on Camino del Monte Sol which her fifteen-year-old daughter and Nella, their canny Spanish-American maid, had been running with the authority of Mothers Superior. Amusing moments ensued when neither of them wished to yield any of that authority to the lay mother; but soon life continued around Big Alice very much as it had done farther up the hill: intimate gatherings, tea, coffee, cigarettes, white mule, and talk, talk, talk. At the sanitarium, we had often read poetry to one another, poetry established and poetry our own. Now, with mainly practitioners present, poetry and painting took fuller sway.

It was a small, pleasant, primitive adobe house, with an outdoor privy and with horses corralled alongside. I remember well when little Starlight was foaled on a cold night. Visitors would come across distances which now demand motoring; but we came on horseback then by day or at night on foot with lanterns and would kick snow off our overshoes in the welcoming glow of the room with its corner adobe fireplace. Painters from near-by houses on the Camino would be there, Applegate, Bakos, Shuster, Nash, sometimes Sloan and Davey from streets farther away, often Indian painters like Awa-tsireh from the Pueblos and occasionally a visiting writer, Lindsay with his chants, Sandburg with his guitar, Frost with his wit, Lummis with a red bandanna round his gray temples, or neighboring Jack Thorpe with his brother.

The Hendersons and I attended many Pueblo ceremonials together in those days; but we liked to watch singly and to absorb the dances, or to be absorbed by them, rather than to make them the social occasions they are now; and when the Easter dance or the August dance came at Santo Domingo, each lasting three days, we would last the three days with them, sleeping on the schoolhouse floor, and be up at dawn to see the first Koshare, with Alice Corbin as alert and hardy as any of us. Sometimes we were the only white watchers. Sometimes we took with us a visiting writer like Bliss Carman or Edna Millay, or a composer like Ernest Bloch.

Resident writers in 1923 were few. Elizabeth Shepley Sargeant was here, telling in *Harper's* about her "mud house"—whence dated, I think, the local dubbing of us painters and writers as "mud-hut nuts."

Manuel Chavez was here, but not yet called Fray Angelico. Mabel Sterne was in Taos but not yet known for her memoirs. Erna Fergusson was in Albuquerque but was conducting tourists to the Indian country, not yet a courier in print. Ruth Laughlin's pen was not yet notably busy. Mary Austin, Haniel Long, Lynn Riggs, Ernest Seton, Oliver La Farge, Alfred Kreymborg, Paul Rosenfeld, Arthur Davison Ficke, Raymond Holden, Louise Bogan, Clifton Fadiman, John Gould Fletcher, and others came later to settle or sojourn in Santa Fe. But Spud Johnson shared my house in 1922, and it was then that the D. H. Lawrences made their first Santa Fe visit. Mabel Sterne, now Mabel Luhan, was bringing them through town from Lamy on their way to visit her in Taos, but it was too late for them to undertake what used to be a long and tough drive. At quick notice she could find no Santa Fe roof for them but mine, although at that time it covered only three small rooms, porous to the wind.

But what a sudden warmth we whipped together—Lorenzo and Frieda, Mabel and Tony Luhan, Alice Corbin, Willy Henderson and Little Alice, Spud and I. Mabel and Tony left early; but the rest of us talked by the fireplace into the snuggest of the small hours, all of us bobbing at Alice as children bob at apples on Hallowe'en. She looked like an apple, with her round, rosy cheeks. And Willy was drawling his narratives of earlier Western days. And Little Alice was correcting both parents at intervals. The Lawrences, tired after their journey from the Coast but relieved to find a simple household, were soon recounting global adventures and they were as much like children as were the rest of us. With the Hendersons' help we gave them a late supper, and Spud and I were up early next morning to wash the dishes and feed our guests; but the Lawrences, let me record, were up before us and every dish was either clean or holding part of a good, hot breakfast which they had prepared and exactly timed for their hosts.

Later, when other writers and multiplying summer visitors came to Santa Fe, Alice Corbin was a main organizer of the annual Poets' Round-Up, to raise funds for Indian causes; and, in closer bound and bond, she brought a small group of us residents together to read and criticize one another's poems and to stimulate new writing: Spud Johnson, Haniel Long, Clifford McCarthy, Lynn Riggs, Robert Hunt and me, with others occasionally joining. Sometimes there would be personal poems betwixt us, a challenge and an answer; and, since Alice Corbin is not to know beforehand that we offer her herewith a garland of respectful affection and therefore can not be asked to grant me the right to print a sonnet of hers, I venture, without her permission to enter a brace of exchange which dates from those poetry meetings. Alice wrote:

EL CONQUISTADOR

You are so much to every casual friend—
The butcher and the baker and the rest,
And anyone who has a mood to spend
May spend it in the hollow of your breast:
Lowitsky has a share in you and all,
All, all possess you—and I only groan
To see you thus made common carnival,
And nothing left for me to call my own!

O Hal, O Hell—what is the use to sue
The insubstantial, evanescent you!
Harlot of sympathies although you be,
I search and hope and never may be sure
If what you give me differs from the lure
That holds Lowitsky and that maddens me!

I replied at the next session of our group:

TO ONE WHO EXCLAIMS AT
MY FRIENDSHIP WITH A
SECOND-HAND DEALER
("You always like anyone.")

Lowitsky breathes his portion of the sky,
He too a curious vessel in the sun,
Of bright afflatus and opinion,
With as good veins to hold them in as I.
Why then pretend that he can only buy
And sell mean objects and perforce be done
With other thinking and with other fun?

Man has a second hand if the first die.

All men are made of earth to comprehend
Sun, moon and stars and thoughts: diameters
Crossing the wheel. Circumference encloses
You, me, Lowitsky too. Unto one end
We move together, while the circle stirs
With all its knowledge and with all its noses.

This sort of interchange was good teasing, good questioning, good fun. I wish it had continued longer. Alice's sonnet, femininely playful, and mine, masculinely pontifical, were not, for others, of any special import in content or expression but for us, in personal and literary stimulus, they were of timely import; and that sort of give and take enlivened our enjoyment and experiment. It was good for us; and Alice managed continuance of our meetings as long as she could. It was not her fault that they ceased, nor was it ours. Towns grow too large. Nor should this particular verse exchange have ended where it did. My pulpit sonnet was not fair. Alice's understanding of every sort of person, her sympathetic entrance into the feelings and reasons of others, have been a lifelong characteristic. Years ago, as everyone knows, she was Associate Editor, with Harriet Monroe as Editor, of *Poetry: a Magazine of Verse*—in fact she was co-founder of it. And in that golden period of American poetry her vivid, sympathetic spirit meant much to most of the poets who made it golden, as it has meant much to all of us who have encountered her in poetry or in life.

Among my letters through the years from Ezra Pound I have found a pertinent passage:
"Alice was only intelligent element (in that frying pan) 1911-12 or whenever—only means of getting an idea into dear ole 'Arriet's hickory block. In short Alice my only comfort during that struggle. Blessings upon her."

Blessings upon her, say we all.

A NOTE ON ALICE CORBIN HENDERSON AND POETRY
George Dillon

"All young poets hate editors," Alice Corbin Henderson once observed in an editorial. "And they are right. When a poet becomes tolerant of an editor, or an editor of a poet, it is not a healthy sign; both have ceased to be alert.... But the established poet, whose reputation is not only made but embalmed, and the editor who has no more plasticity than a hitching post—there is no friction between them. They are mutually tolerant of one another. Why not? The relation between them is simply that of a manufacturer and a retailer of any reasonable staple commodity, like sugar or molasses or green cheese.... All the poet in me hates the editor. The editor in me swears that I am a very bad poet; the poet knows that the editor is a fool. And neither one is entirely wrong."

No doubt it was characteristic of Mrs. Henderson that, having schemed, labored, and exhorted for several years to stir up a new poetry movement, she was quite ready to abandon her dominant role as an editor as soon as the movement showed signs of being a "popular" success. For so it did, momentarily, although young poets today find it hard to believe that anything of the sort happened—the vogue extended into the 1920's, helped along by the same kind of fad excitement that has more recently operated towards the popularization of modern painting. It seemed, for a while, that publishers were bringing out several "leading" or "major" poets every month; and all this uncritical fanfare must have been profoundly boring to Mrs. Henderson, who had recognized and encouraged, when they were altogether unknown, such poets as Pound, Eliot, D. H. Lawrence, Sandburg, and Lindsay.

There were, to be sure, other factors tending to withdraw her from the editorial work, among them her change of residence to New Mexico and her increasing absorption in the lives and culture of the southwestern Indians. That interest was to find expression in a number of singularly real and moving poems, poems deeper and stronger yet simpler than any she had written before. They proved that Mrs. Henderson, whose agile mind and exceptional background enabled her to analyze the masterpieces of literature and to debate subtleties with the best critics alive, had nevertheless found a superior charm and reality in that relatively untouched field of experience. As a poet, she fulfilled her talent in writing about that little-understood minority. Such poems as "On the Acequia Madre" and "Una Anciana Mexicana" have a more lasting quality, it seems to me than a great deal of contemporary work which today is much better known.

It is clear, at any rate, that she had no wish to become a "hitching post for established poets." The editorial from which I have quoted was written in 1916, after four years of intensive service as an editor, during which she, equally with Harriet Monroe and Ezra Pound, had worked to make *Poetry* the protagonist of the new movement. She had also collaborated with Miss Monroe on an anthology which was to become a sort of hieratic best-seller for many years. That she had, however, no illusions about the momentary boom in poetry is evident from a letter sent from New Mexico, at about this time, to her fellow editor:

"Out here, against these hills and in quietness, one is apt to get a perspective on many things. (I've tried to forget the magazine, but I don't succeed.) I very much fear that Cinderella is going back to her ashes, and that she may feel more comfortable there than in her automobile—that this supposed popularity of the art is a good deal of dust, or rather, that when the dust clears away, not much may remain. By that I mean especially that one sees so much stuff passing itself off as poetry that is nothing of the sort. The need for a perfectly fearless high standard was never greater than it is at the moment." And though she expressed pleasure in the new anthology, a copy of which had just arrived, she was candid enough to recognize "some stuff that has no business there at all (including some of mine)."

Mrs. Henderson left Chicago thirty-three years ago, which was just seven years before I came here as a student. I did not know her. Yet as I write the words I am hardly convinced by them, for in those days I was impressionable, and her memory was a recent and vivid one among some of the people I knew—at the magazine and at the university Poetry Club, at Mrs. William Vaughn Moody's, and among those who had been active in the Chicago Little Theatre. I had then no clear appreciation of what she had accomplished—the very large gift of love and intellect which she brought to the establishment of a poet's review. But I was certainly aware of her as a personality; she existed in my imagination (along with

xxix

Elizabeth Roberts, Glenway Westcott, and Yvor Winters) as one of the talented writers who had recently come and gone. Eunice Tietjens spoke of her with devotion. Maurice Lesemann, the young poet whom I most admired, used to read her poems in the unnerving *sostenuto* which we all tried to imitate for he, in a high, unrequited way, had fallen in love with her.

And in the magazine collection there were several photographs of her, looking rather angry and decidedly attractive, which have always startled me with their aliveness.

After leaving Chicago she continued for six years, until 1922, to be a very frequent contributor of editorials and criticism, and a constant adviser to *Poetry*. During these years the continued appearance of her name on the masthead, which both she and Harriet Monroe seemed to regard as an honorary sign, was in fact brilliantly justified. In her letters to Miss Monroe (a rich file, now part of the University of Chicago collection) one can see how frequently she was consulted on manuscripts, books, details of policy; and from the marginal notes in Miss Monroe's handwriting one sees how important her influence was. Even her most lightly humorous remarks were aimed at upholding the "perfectly fearless high standard." There were to be no compromises! "Keep *Poetry* up, up!" she wrote. "The need is all the greater because the other magazines are so poor—you don't want to be classed with them. I shiver when I think of the leftovers in the file! Are there many?"

Here and there, in the letters, certain especially incisive passages have been marked by Miss Monroe as ideas for future development, and in reading the magazine one finds that Mrs. Henderson did develop some of them in the form of editorials; for instance, her excellent piece on impressionistic criticism, "A Jitney Bus among Masterpieces." Those early volumes of *Poetry* make good reading today, a considerable amount of their liveliness being due to the articles signed E. P. and A. C. H. In the light of subsequent history they are often fascinating: one is struck by so many accurate judgments of writers, including British and French poets, who were then unknown or misevaluated—judgments, and comparisons, which must have been regarded as daring and extreme, if not eccentric, at the time, but which now appear to have been simply oracular. The continued life of these articles is also a matter of personality.

Both Pound and Mrs. Henderson commanded a vigorous, informal style which has the quality of good talk; it would be equally refreshing in any of the current literary magazines. At that time Pound was really enjoying himself, writing his keenest criticism, and from the articles and letters of the two writers, it seems clear, that he was very greatly stimulated by the young editor's interest. It was a case of mutual stimulation.

Edith Franklin Wyatt recalls that Mrs. Henderson's admiration of Pound was closely related to her still earlier enthusiasm for Whistler. She felt that Pound would perform the same kind of service for literature that Whistler had done for painting; and she saw various personal analogies between the two men.

I imagine that anyone who has edited *Poetry* in the later years must have come to know the writings of Mrs. Henderson rather well. She is one of those to whom we turn voluntarily (in contrast to most of our dutiful peering into the archives, which has come to be such a large part of the work here). We have turned to her in moments of difficulty and in moments of leisure. We have found courage, the kind we often need, in her criticism—beginning with her early slam of a Masefield book (then widely praised) on the score of facile melodrama. That criticism, of a poet whose best work she admired, is the model of a courageous slam. It appeared in the same issue with Pound's review of *A Boy's Will*. We have also had good counsel from her on the subject of criticism itself. "Criticism," she wrote, "that weighs and balances only after the event is, indeed, of little consequence to the artist. The only criticism of value [to him] is contemporaneous criticism, the kind that is perfectly able to navigate in an uncharted sea, take soundings, and proclaim new depths and shores." We have been entertained by her informal notes and comments (as, for instance, when she quotes several poems from an *Others* anthology, and concludes: "We regret to say the printer announces there are no more I's in the font.") And we have been cheered and strengthened by her consistent refusal to expostulate with, or be baited by, the type of mentality that proposes to edify the arts. In announcing a prize offered by the old *Life* magazine for "a song of modern Democracy, typifying the spirit of Liberty, Fraternity, Equality and the Allies," she remarked simply, "Isn't that enough to frighten the Muse?" The comment serves for all such attempts at forcible inspiration, including the latest I have just heard about: an offer of one thousand dollars for a poem on "Individual and International Morality."

But soon I shall be pulling down, one after another, the volumes of *Poetry* in their worn green bindings—the color Mrs. Henderson chose for them, against angry protests. I must not begin to do that, however, for a selection of even the most memorable passages from her editorial writings would fill another volume. It will be the task of the biographer and literary historian to rediscover all that material and evaluate her contribution to the modern poetry movement and to the magazine. As far as I am concerned, it is quite inestimable. Though she has been away so long, I hope she may find it agreeable to reflect that her mind is a living presence in this office, and will surely continue to be, so long as the doors of *Poetry* remain open.

ALICE CORBIN AND IMAGISM
John Gould Fletcher

The business of poetry is not to teach, or to reflect, but to state—so thought a small group of poets who assembled under the instigation, guidance, and control of the twenty-six year old student of philosophy and art, Thomas Ernest Hulme, at a restaurant in Central London in the early months of the year 1909. Eight years later, Hulme himself was dead in France, his major work unwritten or existing only in brilliant fragments; the notion of poetry that he had been the first to develop had been elaborated and taken up under the name of Imagism by a whole school, led by Ezra Pound in England and Amy Lowell in America; a magazine founded in Chicago by Harriet Monroe had, for five years, been the leading exponent of the revolutionary ideas and technique of Imagism; and the first associate editor of that magazine, the subject of this article, had come to New Mexico to recover from tuberculosis and to write a book of poems which still, in its own way, is a classic example of what was originally meant by Imagism.

Such, and summarily, is the story of Alice Corbin, whose books, along with those of Mary Austin, must forever stand at the forefront of any discussion or critical study that can be made of American literature as it has developed in New Mexico. To transpose the range and feeling of New Mexico into the English language required a handling of style and vocabulary that is not particularly familiar to most Anglo-Saxon writers. It is quite possible to assert—and perhaps it has been asserted by some—that all literature in New Mexico should really be written in Spanish, but inasmuch as the Anglo-Saxon variety of Americans have controlled this region, politically and economically, for a century, to complain that New Mexican literature has largely been written in English is like complaining that W. B. Yeats in Ireland did not write in Gaelic.

Two women, both previously developed as writers by other environments, both highly sensitized as individuals, and neither particularly strong physically, led the way into the foreign-rhythmed, wide-horizoned region of New Mexico. Later on an uprooted Englishman, D. H. Lawrence, who was also intensely sensitive to the feminine side of experience, followed them. It may be said that all three were in a measure influenced by Imagism; or, in the case of Mary Austin, by such direct, objective parallels to Imagism as can be found in American Indian poetry. All three said something about New Mexico that finally had to be said.

Mother earth—*tierra madre*—is what the Spanish-Americans call it; and in that phrase is so much that most Anglo-Saxons cannot understand. In New Mexico, mother earth is most often a harsh mother, since so much is desert—endless gray chamisa and sage looming beyond the narrow spaces of ditch-watered alfalfa, the round orange-gold of pumpkins, the white plumes of corn. Beyond that, the piñon and juniper standing in dense, dark green clumps, still on the desert, but leading the eye to seek for the vast pueblo ruin on the mesa-edge beyond. This last stands as a reminder that there is something here that was old long before the Spaniards raised their crosses and low adobe chapels and farmhouses by the edge of the stream—a people in whose myths the earth was never created at all, but has, despite floods and disasters, always existed. Beyond the piñon and the juniper, the high upland of the rocks and pines—and those strange trees, the aspens, with dull green leaves forever quivering by silvery-grey stems—and then, the bare rock in the cloud, and the snow. Layer on layer of mother-earth and all of it strange: as strange, faraway, remote, and fiercely individual as China or North Africa. And never, despite the throngs forever coming on, of sensation-gaping Eastern tourists, or of untalkative, oddly-detached atomic scientists, coming in from the great laboratory at Los Alamos, can New Mexico be anything else than mother-earth in this sense. Break a branch of piñon and let its resinous sap stick to your fingers, or dig a new water-ditch through this crumbling red soil if you would know why New Mexico earth is mother-earth. It clings as it yields.

Alice Corbin became, along with Mary Austin, one of the two first interpreters—except for a few anthropologists like Gushing and Washington Matthews, who had stuck to the Indian and avoided the Spanish-American element—of New Mexican life in American literature, because Alice Corbin had tried for so long to be a poet, had been taken up in 1912 by Harriet Monroe (a splendid organizer, but not the most sensitive or intellectually daring of editors) as her chief counsellor and assistant; and because Alice Corbin had thus fallen under the influence of Imagism without having met anyone directly connected with the movement. In letter after letter, objection piled on objection, *Poetry*'s first foreign correspondent, the most radical and most disturbing of all the expatriates, Ezra Pound, had hammered away at the new magazine (the first in American history to give prizes to poets) with arguments insisting that everything must be treated directly, objectively, without circumlocutions or inversions of any kind, shorn of all decorative adjectives and windy rhetoric. Although Pound himself went later out of his way to commend the work of another expatriate, T. S. Eliot, whose early poetry seemed to reflect, in a more world-weary fashion, the hyper-aestheticism of the "art-for-art's-sake" people, and such poets as the forgotten Donald Evans, through an atmosphere of even stronger *fin-de-siecle* disillusion, yet Pound's own poetry was not of that sort— but rather tensely primitive or savagely satiric. And Alice Corbin had responded, as later on Miss Monroe's second associate, Eunice Tietjens, also responded, in kind. Perhaps the two most remarkable offshoots of the Imagist movement, apart from D. H. Lawrence, who developed and practised his own kind of imagism, are to this day the books, *Profiles from China*, which Miss Tietjens later published, and Alice Corbin's *Red Earth* which appeared in 1920. And both are by-products of the atmosphere manifest in *Poetry*'s Chicago office.

Red Earth is a book of individual portraits, as the prose *Brothers of Light* later on is a book of scenes and backgrounds. There is nothing in it that does not belong to New Mexico, and it stands to this day as the best book of direct, objective New Mexican poetry written in English. It has all the sharpness of that unforgettable landmark among American poetry books, Edgar Lee Masters' *Spoon River Anthology*. But it is better written, with a deeper sense of the poetical apprehension of experience, and less externalism and surface reporting. A few examples reveal how close it is to its sources in Imagist poetry. "In the Desert" starts like this:

> I have seen you, O king of the dead,
> More beautiful than sunlight.
>
> Your kiss is like quicksilver;
> But I turned my face aside
> Lest you should touch my lips.
>
> In the field with the flowers
> You stood darkly.

This is, in rhythm and in handling (note the development of the cadence and the absence of adjectives) clearly derived from the Imagist H. D.:

> You are clear,
> O rose, cut in rock;
> Hard as the descent of hail.

and also:

> The light beats upon me,
> 1 am startled.
> A split leaf crackles on the paved floor;
> I am anguished—defeated.

"Juan Quintana" pursues the same line of approach, along with a quality of folk-portrayal taken from Yeats and from other Irish poets, such as Padraic Colum, of Yeats' following:

> The goat-herd follows his flock
> Over the sandy plain,
> And the goats nibble the rabbit-brush
> Acrid with desert rain.
>
> Old Juan Quintana's coat
> Is a faded purple blue,
> And his hat is a worn brown;
> And his trousers a tawny hue.
>
> He is sunburnt like the hills,
> And his eyes have a strange goat look.

Yeats himself would have recognized that as a poem of his own vintage, far more easily than he did the outwardly more ambitious but inwardly far more self-consciously orchestral folk-balladry of Vachel Lindsay.

"Una Anciana Mexicana" is in blank verse, with conversational overtones that recall some of Ezra Pound's own best early poems as well as those of Robert Frost:

> I've seen her pass with eyes upon the road—
> An old bent woman in a bronze-black shawl,
> With skin as brown and wrinkled as a mummy's,
> As brown as a cigar-box, and her voice
> Like the low, vibrant strings of a guitar.

Here, in three different poetic modes (cadenced verse, ballad, blank verse) is the gist of Alice Corbin's vision of New Mexico—a vision strangely objective, direct, unwavering, without either speculative self-analysis or sentimental self-pity:

> When it's all over and there's none to care,
> I mean to be like her and take my share
> Of comfort when the bright day's done,
> And smoke away the nights and see the sun
> Through eyes that open inward and look back.

Which again recalls Yeats in his most realistic vein as well as Pound.

What was it, then, that had attracted Alice Corbin so powerfully to the "New Poetry" practiced by mid-western realists, Irish folk- and myth-singers, and to the as yet as good as unknown group of Imagists developing under Hulme and Pound and Flint in London? She had taken the liberty of writing to Pound direct in the summer of 1912 (eight years before *Red Earth* was published) and had asked him to contribute to the new magazine which Harriet Monroe was now publishing. How had she even heard of the name—unforgettable now, whether for good or evil—of Ezra Pound, who so far had scarcely even been published in the United States, and who had come back to this country but briefly in 1911-12, since his first departure in 1908? Is it possible that she had heard of Pound through Yeats, who may have been interested from the days when Pound, in 1909, had shaken the complacency of Edwardian London with his *Personae and Exhortations*? I do not know the answer to that question, and perhaps Alice Corbin does not recall how it happened that the Imagists entered the columns of Poetry from the date of the first number in 1912. In any case, all we can say is, that without their influence, without the influence of Pound, H. D., Aldington, Flint—the poems contained in *Red Earth* could not have been written. Nor would *Poetry* have marked so sharp a break from Victorian tradition.

New Mexico itself, with its sharp contrasts of landscape and of life, gave the technique which produced one of the best regional books written in America over the last thirty years.

That such a development of Imagism as *Red Earth* shows that Imagism was, after all, capable of producing poetry of only limited range is a truism today. The poetry that has had a wider following since that time has sprung from a disquiet concerning man and his destiny that was set going by Eliot's *Waste Land* in 1922, and which moves back to such sources in speculation and in poetry as Marlowe, Webster, Donne, Pascal, Baudelaire, and Rimbaud. None of the critics who have so voluminously and exhaustively argued about this newer, more "metaphysical" type of poetry, have as yet been able to say whether the metaphor which takes the central place in this type of verse, as "the image" did in the earlier verse as an "objective correlative" of the emotion, is actually a kind of knowledge, non-scientific but complete, or merely a personal game of the poet, playing with his own private association of thought. Thus the earlier, more imagistic poetry, which aimed at less, and actually achieved more, may be said to possess a more valid claim to permanence.

These considerations of structure and texture, which have made present-day American poetry more formal on the surface, but far more complex in its desperate shifts from abstract logic to far-fetched detail, were foreign to all the first Imagists, to Hulme, to Pound, to H. D., to Flint, to Aldington, to myself. The business of the poet then was not to teach, not to provide an "apprehension of experience" or an "objective correlation of emotion," but to observe and restate historic and objective reality. The language and the thing were then one, in such poetry as Alice Corbin wrote in her *Red Earth*. And her *Brothers of Light*, the prose book she did on the Penitentes, has equally the objectivity, the directness of good Imagism. Compared with these, the poems collected in *The Sun Turns West* reveal a writer with a deeper quality of mysticism, with more inwardness possibly, but also one less sure of her ground, more given to Celtic indefiniteness.

THREE POEMS
Alice Corbin

LINES

Love and remorse
Struggle to keep me
Wondering why
Peace cannot come without sorrow—
And sorrow drown
Remembrance.

TESUQUE GARDEN

Now is the season of
bending down
To the earth,
the sweet earth—
Planting the seed,
feeling the bud—
Coaxing with love
the pliant earth—
Now is the season
of earth and love.

EDGAR

The sunlight was about him always:
And at high noon
He was lifted like a ray to the Source
of all Light...
Remembering, we remember ever
How the air always brightened where he walked:

Remembering, we remember ever
How he lived in that Light.

ALICE
Carl Sandburg

"Alice Corbin, where art thou?" runs a query often in the minds and memories of the Old Guard who witnessed the launching of *Poetry: a Magazine of Verse* in 1912. She had a gallant heart and a gay smile and the great expectations required for the sailing of that dauntless little ship. A poet, a creative critic and editor, she has a definite and highlighted place in the story of American literature of that period. When some of us arrive at where we can with ease look backward and record with care and deliberation certain adventures we have seen and shared, Alice Corbin will stand forth in elements of both the angelic and the demoniac. Only one having both those elements could have the range of affectionate understanding, compassion through identity, necessary to ride herd on Vachel and Carl, Edgar Lee and Ezra, Robinson and Hal Bynner, H. D. and Amy, John Gould Fletcher and Edwin Arlington Robinson, those two lawyers Archie MacLeish and Wally Stevens—and God knows who all, by the way of clowns, acrobats, trapeze artists, sword swallowers and fire eaters. "Alice Corbin, where art thou?" Whithersoever thou art, if you ain't got sweet reminiscences, who has?

ALICE CORBIN
Padraic Colum

Reversing Aristotle I now measure time by movements. So it was at the time when Chicago was the center of American literary activity, when *Poetry* was making Poets and Poems important, and when Vachel Lindsay, still with Nicholas preceding his name, was making crowds join in those recitations of his so enchantingly filled with sound and color, when visitors could find signs that works and figures of Renaissance proportions were going to have their births in Chicago, that, in a studio or drawing room I would become aware of a young woman's looks and words.

As she was one of the editors of I and the wife of a painter with ideas, what she said generally was expectedly authoritative. But that was not remembered by me. Then sometimes she would say something with an odd intentness and an odd reserve. It is by these momentary withdrawals and tentative movements that Alice Corbin stays in my mind as someone who had known something the recollection of which would bring gentleness into her looks.

In a poem that Ezra Pound quoted as one of the best written in that epoch, the text of which I cannot now find, what was recollected by her came to me. It was a short poem about some bare, sun-dried place and the lost hope and glory that belonged to one who looked over it, one of those Castilians whom nothing in our civilization can help us to understand. But she understood and could speak for the man. What she had to say was not about the glory of the Conquistador but about a dream that was eclipsed, not by soldiery from another side but by the days of the modern and the way of the world. Her recollection is of a dream that is eclipsed.

Her lost dream has a Spaniard to characterize it:

The old songs
Die—
And the lips that sang them.
Wreathed, withered and dusty,
Cuff-buttons with royal insignia
There, in the musty museum,
Are all that is left of Sarasate.

Somewhere, somehow, sometime, Alice Corbin got the endowment that is so rare in American poets, the endowment of reverie, and it is reverie that gives distinction to certain of her poems and brings them close to the folk-song with its thoughtfulness:

But would you stay as now you are
Or as a year ago?
Oh, not as then, for then how small
The wisdom we did owe!
Or if forever as today
How little we could know!

When I read the poem that this verse is in over to myself, I understand how that young woman with brown hair and brown eyes and a heart-shaped face moved me by some words said tentatively, said intently, said with reserve.

SANTA FE IN THE TWENTIES
Ruth Laughlin

I always think of the William Penhallow Hendersons as smiling; of Whippie stalking along in high-heeled boots, eyes twinkling under his big sombrero, small moustache widened in a grin and a merry quip for me as we passed; of the smile that lifted Alice Corbin's round, red cheeks and shone deeply in her brown eyes. Through a friendship of more than thirty years it is good to recall those smiling faces. The smiles were never fatuous or merely polite. They expressed deep humor and courage and the inner resources of creative artists who faced life with high challenge and a gay curiosity as to what would happen next.

One day last fall, when the cottonwoods on the Tesuque hillside below her house were shining gold, Alice Corbin and I laughed over the memories of Santa Fe in the 1920's.

"Years ago you told me that only the newcomer should write of the Southwest," I reminded Alice. "You said that first impressions were clear, vivid and exciting but that after six months the scene became too familiar and lost its sharp focus."

"I've changed my time limit on that," she laughed, "though the memory of my first Christmas in Santa Fe is so vivid that I can almost feel the crisp cold air now. We came here in 1916 and I have written about the impact of New Mexico ever since. There is still much that I want to say...."

"Your poems in the *Turquoise Trail* and *Red Earth* express what all of us would like to say about this country," I said.

"We loved this Red Earth country from the beginning, even though we came here for my health," Alice explained. "We wanted to see all of it ... every pueblo, every Indian dance, every Spanish village. We rode horseback to Chimayo and stayed all night with Mr. Chavez whose family built the Sanctuario long ago as their private chapel. That was during the First World War and the little statue of Santiago wore a tin lemon sieve on his head, bent to look like a war helmet. His arm was broken and Willie mended it with tissue paper and glue."

That act of helping to save a prized relic was typical of the Hendersons. They valued the historic traditions of Santa Fe and worked to preserve them. They took a vital interest in the town and supported every worthy civic project whether it was concerned with art, architecture, writing, the Fiesta, or a water trough for thirsty horses hitched near the plaza.

Alice Corbin spent her first year at Sunmount Sanitarium, and Whippie and the small daughter Alice lived in a near-by adobe house on the loma south of town. When Alice moved down to join them she discovered that the rutted dirt road in front of their home was called Telephone Road in honor of the proud new telephone poles marching up the hill. She changed that to the original Spanish name, El Camino del Monte Sol, the Road to the Sun Mountain. Other artists and writers soon built their studios near the Hendersons and the Camino became famous, but I always think of the name as a monument to the poetic sensitiveness of Alice Corbin.

In our busy lives the years pass rapidly and mostly without specific dates or events. It was my visit with Alice Corbin and my realization of what she had meant to Santa Fe that brought me a fresh evaluation of the last three decades. At the close of the 1940's I realize that many members of the original art colony have passed on, others have reached distinguished maturity in spite of the devastating years of World War II, and a new group is now adding vitality to the old town. I think of the 1930's as the depression years when many plans were thwarted but also as a period when the art colony settled in and became an integral part of Santa Fe. I look back to the 1920's as an astonishing decade that flourished with initial impetus, creative urge and significant civic development.

Early in the twentieth century the fame of the Taos Art Colony encouraged many young artists to come to the Southwest instead of Paris. Santa Fe's pioneer artists were Kenneth Chapman and Carlos Vierra, followed in 1912 by Gerald and Ina Sizer Cassidy. During the next eighteen years probably no art colony in the United States had a more active roster than Santa Fe. The artists in permanent residence included W. P. Henderson, Warren Rollins, Albert Schmidt, Sheldon Parsons, Gustave Baumann, Olive Rush, Raymond Jonson, B. J. O. Norfeldt, Dorothy Stewart, Henry Balink, Preston McCrossen, Datus Myers, Andrew Dasburg, Vernon Hunter, Theodore Van Soelen, John Sloan, Randall Davey, Julius Rohlshoven, McHarg Davenport, William Lumpkins, Frank Applegate, Josef Bakos, Fremont Ellis, Willard Nash, Will Shuster, Walter Mruk and three sculptors, Eugenie Shonnard, Allan Clark and George Blodgett. Among the writers were Alice Corbin, Mary Austin, Witter Bynner, Willard Johnson, Haniel Long, Ida Raugh, Glenway Westcott, Lynn Riggs, Isabel Campbell, Elizabeth De Huff, Ruth Laughlin, Omar Barker, Roark Bradford, Earl and Marion Scott, Dorothy Hughes, John Curtis Underwood, Peggy Pond Church, Ray Otis, Phillip E. Stevenson, Thomas Wood Stevens and Helen Stevens.

In the 1920's Santa Fe was a small, friendly town where everyone knew everyone else and each individual's work was a valuable asset to the community. Whippie Henderson painted the murals for the Country Club where we danced, and Gerald Cassidy painted the murals for the movie theatre. The Little Theatre had enthusiastic members including Jane Baumann, Anna V. Huey, Hazel Pond, Norman Magee, Edwin Brooks, John Evans, Jim Macmillan and Robert Brown. Ashley Pond slid down a pole from his bedroom to his garage to jump in his car, race to a burning building and lead the Volunteer Fire Department whose staff numbered several artists and professional men.

During those years Lynn Riggs wrote his first one-act play called *Knives From Syria* with the encouragement of Ida Raugh. Glenway Westcott and Ted Stevenson struggled with their first novels, Mary Austin wrote books and articles, exhorted audiences and presided in Buddha-like majesty over a young crop of writers jokingly called the Genius Club. Marsden Hartley found inspiration in New Mexico's primitive religious art and wrote sensitive interpretations of Indian ceremonies. Poets gathered around Alice Corbin and Witter Bynner, and Spud Johnson published their poems in his temperamentally gaited literary magazine, *The Laughing Horse*.

Frank Applegate stopped over on a cross-country trek and stayed the rest of his life. His versatile gifts included ceramics, painting, writing, and collecting primitive art in bultos and santos. He bought land on the Camino opposite the Hendersons and encouraged a group of young artists to mix adobes and build their homes on that hillside. They called themselves the Cinco Pintores, the five painters being Will Shuster, Josef Bakos, Willard Nash, Fremont Ellis and Walter Mruk. These artists delighted in the plastic lines of adobe architecture but the sloping lintels of Mruk's house even went beyond the local vagaries. For years his place was known as the "Adam and Eve House" on account of the colossal nude figures moulded on the street side of his fireplace. Across the road Mary Austin began to build her "Beloved House" and below her Alice and Datus Myers completed a spacious home with tiled walls, patios and fountains, studios and library. By this time the Hendersons had added rooms and studios to their vanguard adobe home.

Outside these simple mud houses conformed to traditional Spanish-Indian lines, but inside the artists expressed their individual tastes. Witter Bynner installed his fine Chinese carvings, paintings and jade in his adobe home. John Sloan painted the geometric lines of Indian design on his floors and ceilings. Gus Baumann carved lintels and doorways with the skill he had long used for wood-block prints. The etcher in B. J. O. Nordfelt found expression in the carved and gilded panels set into his ceiling. Randall Davey restored a Spanish balcony on his house at the end of Canyon Road, and Theodore Van Soelen and Albert Schmidt built homes at Tesuque. Olive Rush, Sheldon Parsons, and Gerald and Ina Cassidy bought historic houses on Canyon Road and added carved beams, church panels and patio gardens.

No one took as intense an interest in Spanish-Indian architecture as Carlos Vierra. He studied and photographed every old building he could find and preached his gospel of the long heritage of native architecture so vehemently that it became known as the "Santa Fe Style," although buildings at the State University in Albuquerque had been designed along Indian lines some years before.

The archaeologist, Sylvanus Griswold Morley, was the first to restore an old adobe for his home and show that native construction and carving was more attractive than the new-fangled red brick bungalows. Fired by the enthusiasm of Sylvanus Morley and Carlos Vierra that generous patron of the arts, the Honorable Frank Springer, gave the first large contribution toward a State Art Museum to be built along the lines of New Mexico's venerable mission churches. Later Mr. Springer commissioned Carlos Vierra to build a new house along the old lines which remains to this day one of the best examples of its kind.

A young architect, who was then a patient at Sunmount, spent days with Carlos Vierra studying old photographs and plans. His name was John Gaw Meem and by 1923 he had designed his first "Santa Fe Style" homes. A few years later the Santa Fe railroad chose him to remodel and enlarge La Fonda Hotel. Since then his name has become synonymous with the best designs of southwestern architecture.

This was the era of the world-wide renaissance of native crafts. It was a revolt against the mechanized destruction of World War I, a nostalgic longing for peace and a hunger for beauty produced by a man's own hands. New Mexico's Indian and Spanish handicrafts assumed new importance in this revival. The art colony led movements to sustain and preserve such indigenous crafts as pottery, silver and tin smithing, embroidery and weaving.

The Hendersons, Mary Austin, Frank Applegate, the Senior and Junior Leonora Curtins, Mary Wheelwright, Frank and Harry Mera, John Gaw Meem and Carlos Vierra, were leaders in organizing the Spanish Colonial Arts Society and the Indian Arts Fund. Through the latter ancient Indian pottery was saved and the best examples of new pottery were added to form a collection that has become an inspiration to international designers and to the modern Indian craftsmen.

The Indian Arts Fund collection of pottery, blankets, baskets and silver was the inspiration for building the Laboratory of Anthropology with financial aid from the Rockefeller Foundation and on land south of town donated by Amelia Elizabeth White and Francis Wilson.

Near the Laboratory Mary Wheelwright planned a unique museum for Navajo Ceremonial Arts. William Penhallow Henderson designed this museum on the lines of a Navajo hogan, and Alice Corbin wrote the text for the Navajo legends explaining the Navajo sand paintings.

The art colony did not closet itself in an adobe tower to paint or write but became articulate and intensely interested citizens. These people had discovered an Old World charm and tranquility in Santa Fe and were determined to preserve it. They fought against tearing down old houses and replacing them with filling stations, against reducing Santa Fe to that ugly American sameness that is labeled Progress, against Texas Club Women who innocently planned a Culture Center. They were individualists who argued violently with each other but united against too much change in their adopted home. Whippie Henderson felt this so strongly that he began to design buildings and planned the restoration of Sena Plaza for Amelia Elizabeth White. Alice Corbin always spoke up at any meeting where the original character of Santa Fe was imperiled.

Human rights as well as civic problems gained a champion in Alice Corbin. She was an original member of an organization formed to defeat the Bursum bill and its threat to pueblo lands. For twenty-five years she has worked with the New Mexico Association on Indian Affairs to help the Indians and encourage their arts and crafts.

As a writer her influence was also widespread and vital. Although she had resigned as associate editor of *Poetry* when she left Chicago, she continued to serve as long-distance adviser and was in touch with numerous poets who submitted their work to that important magazine. When Harriet Monroe, editor of *Poetry*, visited Alice in Santa Fe the local group gathered around the Henderson fireplace and talked far into the night about old and new forms of literature.

Other friends of Alice Corbin came to find out why she was so enthusiastic about an off-the-railroad western town. Witter Bynner planned a three-day stop to see Alice and give a lecture, and became a permanent resident. Bynner took over the adobe house of Paul Berlin, the painter, and his wife Natalie Curtis, who wrote of Indian music. Among others who lived here for part of the year were Arthur Davison Ficke, Edna St. Vincent Millay, Robert Henri, George Bellows and Nicolas Roerick. Willa Cather came here to check material for her classic *Death Comes for the Archbishop*. Alma Gluck sang at informal evenings at the Hendersons, Ernest Bloch composed his American Symphony, and Adolf Bohlm interpreted Russian dances. Sinclair Lewis wandered in and out of studios, Carl Sandburg chanted ballads to his guitar, and Vachel Lindsay gave his inimitable "Chinese Nightingale" as a special treat for his friend Alice Corbin.

Although automobiles did not have modern high-speed motors, other New Mexico writers and artists traveled the dirt roads to join the Santa Fe parties. Mabel Dodge Luhan and Tony, D. H. Lawrence and Frieda, Ernest Blumenschein, Victor Higgins, Howard Cook, Barbara Latham and Kenneth Adams came down from Taos; Erna and Harvey Fergusson came up from Albuquerque, Paul Horgan from Roswell, and Oliver La Farge from field work in the Indian country.

Everyone looked forward to John and Dolly Sloan's annual celebration August 4. One year the Bohemian crowd was startled to see a white horse join the party in the studio. Every year the audience demanded that Hal Bynner repeat his sermon by the Negro preacher, Randall Davey give his hilarious interpretations, and John Sloan go through his act of finding the hair in the soup.

Visiting, talking, partying are essential recreations for artists. Evenings at the Sloans', Hendersons', Hal Bynner's, or Mary Austin's offered exchange of thoughts and often heated arguments. They served as cross-pollenization to fertilize the artist's half-formed plans. I remember one evening when we were all sitting on the floor in front of the fireplace and Dolly whispered, "Don't disturb Sloan. I can see that he is getting an idea for a picture." Between celebrations the art colony did serious work and gained national recognition.

Alice Corbin's appreciation of New Mexico grew deeper each year. She collected a fine library of southwestern books and studied New Mexican history, Indian myths, Penitente rituals and the folk legends and customs of her Spanish-American and Indian neighbors. She was always eager to get first hand information from such authorities as Edgar L. Hewett, Paul A. F. Walter, E. Dana Johnson, Charles F. Lummis, Nina Otero-Warren, Kenneth Chapman and Harry Mera. She delighted in Howard Thorpe's early reminiscences and encouraged him to write his collections of cowboy stories and ballads. She was an enthusiastic friend and admirer of Eugene Manlove Rhodes and, in later years, took the lead in an effort to bring out a memorial edition of all his books and make his grave a literary shrine.

Her generous help for young writers as well as those who have attained distinction has been a fine and lasting influence. Her interest has deepened with thirty years' residence and today she is still eager to add her smiling wisdom and encouragement to any constructive development in the arts or community life. In Santa Fe we value Alice Corbin as a good citizen, a distinguished poet and a beloved neighbor.

THE POETS' ROUND-UP
Haniel Long

Dusk of a day late in February, 1925, Santa Fe. I was going to meet Alice Corbin Henderson for the first time. An old friend was taking me across the mile of fields between his little house and her little house. It was supposed to be a short cut, this march across the fields, for we were late, but barbed wire fences rose up against us. The stars above the white mountains seemed enormous fruit on a lacework of dark limbs and branches. The evening smelt of cedar burning in kitchen stoves. Fresh arborvitae burned on the hearth of Calypso, I remembered. But it was not across the fields of parsley we strode towards Alice Corbin—it was through the barbed wire of modern times. Occasionally my friend groaned; he was a genius for getting caught between the second and third wires.

Then a warm kitchen and Alice Corbin and her daughter, Little Alice, and her husband, "Whippy" (William Penhallow Henderson), a tall man with an iron gray moustache, and twinkling eyes. Nella, the smiling maid had made coffee, lots of it, and there was bread and butter; I had long known of Alice Corbin because she was one of the founders of *Poetry: a Magazine of Verse*. With my wife (another Alice, I was in a world of Alices), I had been studying abroad, and in a French magazine had read some of Alice Corbin's *Red Earth* poems translated by Andre Spire, and it had been my first knowledge of a book that still inspires awe in me. I looked at Alice Corbin in the well lighted, cheerful kitchen and some of the French lines went through my mind; she had written them in French, I conceived, being confused by the unfamiliar region and the new, mysterious people I was meeting. It really doesn't matter in what language the Red Earth poems are written, for they come from the beginning of things, like the large stars over the mountains, like the fragrant arborvitae on the hearth, only they are infinitely melancholy, with the loneliness of the heart at day's end. And they are infinitely remote, as though written by one who saw the world and its doings from a long way off, where only the eternal elements of man's life matter—birth and death, love, suffering. It was the mood in which she had first seen this southwestern country, and there was good reason for it. Reading the Red Earth poems in the atmosphere of postwar Europe, I could respond to their undertones; and reading them today in the bleak world of East-West tension, I respond anew to their impact. The graver the moment in one's personal life or in one's world, the more these poems have to give.

The night I speak of, Alice Corbin was wearing a dust-colored riding skirt and a white blouse and blue sweater, and I mention it because it is the costume I associate her with. Out of doors she added to it a leather jacket and a small, dust-colored squarish sombrero, with a thong under the chin fastened to two Navajo silver buttons she had sewed to her hat—a perfect way of dressing for the Southwest, windy or sunny or snowy.

Alice Corbin had a little study in a field sloping from El Camino del Monte Sol, where the painters lived, down into the nest to the last valley before the rise of the mountains. A wonderful thing it was that Witter Bynner, Spud Johnson, Lynn Riggs and I used to walk over there one evening a week to talk poetry with her, and read new poems. Alice Corbin makes very little difference in the reading of poetry and prose. That was the way with most of us, but Johnson always read very fast and in a low voice and had to be enticed into reading a poem again. Bynner intoned his poems like a bishop the prayerbook; we often asked to read them for ourselves, since it was hardly likely that any poem ever written could be as good as all of his sounded as he read them. When he has thus read my verses, I have been astonished at how well I write, and demanded to see my manuscripts at once. Riggs read well and with real interest in what he had written, and he often held up the palm of his hand as he neared the end as though asking us not to begin sniping till he was through, since the end was the best. He was at that time writing a sonnet a day; as Johnson said, making it not a daily dozen but a daily fourteen.

The small adobe study had a fireplace and a window at each end and a door to the east. It was furnished with enough chairs for us, and had a table. The walls were covered with bookshelves and all the books were books of poems or dealt with poets and poetry. Later we met in other rooms in another house Henderson was building, but we never gathered at anybody else's house for many years. I have always had a special fondness for the adobe room where the books were so near, so quickly picked out and used, and where the moon and the large stars and the winds and odors of fields were a part of our deliberations.

I can give my own account, remembering that the account of any of my associates would be different. Riggs and Johnson generally sat a little apart from the rest of us and did a good deal of talking together, when the manuscripts being examined did not interest them. I would call their attitude neutral but agreeable. They came quickly to the defense of a poem they thought was getting rough treatment. Alice Corbin herself was always a gentle critic, and took the position of allowing a poem to grow in its own right like a plant. Her attitude towards a new poem, or a new aspect of a friend's psyche, was one of welcome.

Nella, the maid, who produced such good coffee, often said to her mistress when things went wrong, "Put no tension to it"; but in our poetry evenings tension there was bound to be, though not too serious.

Alice Corbin is definitely a group person. Several things resulted from these evenings. For example, seven years later, a group of us started a venture in co-operative publishing—an intricate and instructive tale not to be gone into here. More for the general reader is the story of the Poet's Round-Up.

Alice Corbin, Margaret McKittrick, Sarah McComb, and Maurice Leseman were sitting one afternoon in Mrs. McComb's walled garden wondering how they could raise money for the New Mexico Association on Indian Affairs. Alice Corbin proposed public readings by the local poets. Leseman suggested that Margaret McKittrick introduce them and the latter said she would wear her cowboy outfit to do so. "Then it can be a rodeo," someone suggested, "and the poets can be the horses." The summer public was willing to pay money to see the poets, and there are always a good many poets in Santa Fe. And the poets were glad to co-operate to help the Pueblo Indians. Through the stormy time of the Bursum bill and afterwards, the Indians were in need of help, and their defenders were in need of money to help them. It has been true of Santa Fe, from the first entry of Kearny's troops, this interest in the welfare of the peace-loving Pueblo Indians. It is a wistful interest, not without the suggestion that our own evolutionary path has gone too far in the direction of exploitation.

In past ages poets have often faced their public, and it is good for the poets and good for the public to look at one another. In contests in the past laurel wreathes have been prizes. Poets have accompanied themselves on musical instruments. The troubadors recited or sang the songs their jongleurs had written for them. At the Olympic games, poetic contests honored Apollo. But I have not heard of any occasion quite like the Round-Up.

To Alice Corbin, for the sake of performers and audience, the affair had to be given a casual and semi-humorous turn. Being introduced as though they were horses coming out of the chutes at a rodeo took away self-consciousness, and it amused the audience. Before and during the affair, Peach Van Stone (Mrs. Walter Mayer) played the guitar and sang Spanish or cowboy songs. At first we held the Round-Up on the lawn to the north of Sarah McComb's house, under the tall cotton-woods along the river. There was always the fear of rain, for the rains come in summer, and at times we had deluges. There was the whistling of the narrow gauge train from Durango, which traveled at the rate of a fast burro. And there was the wind in the trees to contend with, a poetic rival indeed.

The audience sat on camp chairs arranged as near the chutes as possible, and could hear and understand most of the poems, I hope, despite time and tide and the narrow gauge train. Many of our auditors came back year after year, both residents of Santa Fe and summer visitors.

The performers often included personages like Mary Austin, Langdon Mitchell, Ernest Seton. All of us who were to read would meet at Alice Corbin's the evening before, so that we might arrange a balanced program. It is not as easy as one might think to do so. People love to hear ballads and stories and also witty poems, but we had to have a great deal more variety. Alice Corbin solved the difficulty by insisting that the poet read something in his true vein.

She was never more tactful and casual than in persuading the reluctant, strengthening the timid, advising the confused, and this of course in the midst of general conversation and argument. It was her attitude of welcome to what each of us had to give that made a success of it. Not all poets want to appear in public; not all of them want to dress up in blue jeans or Navajo skirts and jewelry; not all of them have good voices; not all of them, one might say, find life worth living. But the element of competition is excellent, as our kindly governess reminded us; the written word is destined for the eye and mind of others. It is true that the poet is the most independent of all artists, and the only one who can afford to look beyond the questions of what his hearers might find agreeable. But he faces a difficulty of a different kind, quite often, in a natural reluctance at personally reading to the world what he has dragged up from his own insides. All poets are shy, I think, even those who appear otherwise.

And one more thing about Alice Corbin. Once I had to while away a good deal of time doing nothing much, and I used to recite to myself my favorite poets, by the hour. But a poem which had haunted me for years, during the month of March—and it was now March at its worst—one of Pound's, proved irrecoverable except for one line:

"Stepping beneath a boisterous wind from Thrace," . . . I used to ask my friends whether they knew it or knew where I could find it. It is a trivial episode, but at the time, even in a world full of apprehension and suffering, the loss of this poem was a matter of moment to me. This Alice Corbin understood. If others did, they gave no sign of it. It was she who tracked the poem down, typed it off, and gave it to me to put in my wallet. I value this characteristic of Alice Corbin. . . .

She is a group person, as I say; and by that I mean a good deal. She has been part of various good movements here; she is at home in that civic world, and often a leader in it. But there is another kind of group in which I always see Alice Corbin, in which the end is simply to be with friendly spirits who share one's interests and enthusiasms; where people are valued for what they are, it is not a question of whipping them into line. Such groups, naturally unknown in totalitarian states, are the flower of the free nations, and the people who fit into them easily, and fight to save them, are, I often think, our most precious possessions. Fighting to save them may mean many things, but in daily life it means not trying to control the atmosphere of one's group, and not using it as a place to show off. It means paying others an attention full of perceptiveness of them as individuals.

THE RABBLE
Spud Johnson

It all started at the old Henderson house—the little adobe with the deep screened porch at the corner, which stood just above the acequia on El Camino del Monte Sol. This house was perhaps the humblest on the road, yet it always sparkled with warm generosity and always swarmed with celebrities or neighbors, quite indiscriminately.

(Little Alice screaming in Spanish at Nella or her myriad relations; Whippie telling a long, long western yarn while dinner cooled; Alice Corbin smiling benignly at bedlam or at a quiet conversation, with equal calm and keen understanding.)

I remember many evenings there when the after-dinner gaiety was provided by playing a sonnet-writing game which George called "Borymay." Whether this word came into our (or my) language by the Law of Hobson-Jobson from a French word which made sense, I don't know. I have a vague recollection that somebody once said it did.

Anyhow, the game consisted of each person contributing a word, or perhaps two or three, depending upon how many of us were playing. The third and fourth words had to rhyme with the first and second, the seventh and eighth with the fifth and sixth, and so on through fourteen words, to make a Shakespearean sonnet. Then each person wrote his own sonnet, all of us using the identical end-words. Surprisingly enough, we always produced a remarkable variety of compositions: some quite preposterous, of course; a few very apt to be scatological; and occasionally a quite respectable poem.

It was a good game in itself, and proved even better in its effect, for it started all of us into a new frenzy of writing. Soon we were bringing things we had written during the week to try out on each other, or to ask for criticisms and suggestions; and our gatherings tended to become a regular weekly event, and to be limited to writers, rather than a mixed group of painters, summer visitors, musicians and what not.

Alice Corbin had written very little since the publication of *Red Earth*. Little Alice was growing up and then getting married at fifteen; the new house further up the hill on the Camino was being built—everything had conspired to keep her too busy to write verse. So she was delighted, I think, to have us give that little push of incentive that group activity, at its best, can supply so painlessly.

Hal Bynner was then working on the Chinese translations almost exclusively, and he, too, was glad of this slight prod to write more of his own lyrics.

Haniel Long had recently come to Santa Fe, and with him I think it was a kind of relief to be talking shop with writers who were not his students, for he had been teaching for many years at Carnegie Tech.

Lynn Riggs and I completed the group: we were the youngsters, just out of college, and thrilled to be included in a group of professionals who discussed our work as gravely and seriously as they did their own.

So it came about, quite naturally, and with no plan at all, that we were meeting every week, generally at the Hendersons; and before we knew it, we were "A Club."

We were quite serious about it, yet gay, too. It was a workshop group, and we were all using it to try out new things, to get an advance reaction before sending things out into the bleak world of terse rejection slips; and as a stimulus to make us write when we might otherwise have fallen into the good old manana spirit. But sometimes we wrote things just to amuse the group, or to burlesque each other, or simply to fill the gap between more serious "inspirations."

It was in these deviations that Alice was the ringleader. Her eyes sparkled and darkened with a real roguishness when she made some gently naughty crack, or pushed one of us off some too-sententious height with a ladylike but nevertheless bawdy quip, generally in her lowest, most throaty tone, but with an infectious gurgle of laughter behind it.

And that is how we got our name: we seemed to lapse so often into a Rabelaisian mood, that soon we were referring to ourselves as The Rabelais Club, which was quickly altered, since that sounded much too stodgy, to the simple informality of "The Rabble."

It's a little sad to be recalling this now as something that happened a long time ago; but the interesting thing is that the group has not been completely dispersed, and we not only meet frequently and speak often of our old club, but occasionally revive it, with added members.

For instance, all of us, except Riggs, still live in New Mexico and not so many miles apart; and last year he was here again for several months—and, lo, the Rabble rose up on its hind legs and had several pleasant sessions, with three of the founders absent, but with three new members informally added.

And who knows but that verses written at these later gatherings may appear in Alice Corbin's next revised edition of *The Turquoise Trail*, just as the Rabble's first efforts certainly had a prominent place in Alice's own book *The Sun Turns West*, in Hal's *Indian Earth*, Haniel's *Atlantides* or even portions of *Pittsburgh Memorandum*, in Lynn's *The Iron Dish*, and in my *Horizontal Yellow*.

So thank you for all of us, Alice. The Rabble made us jolly—made us write—and it would not have existed but for your gay, hospitable interest in all of us, and in what we were doing.

THE PENITENTE BOOK
Oliver La Farge

So far as I know, there exists only one book upon the Penitentes of New Mexico which one can hand to any interested person with the assurance that it is completely dependable, and that is *Brothers of Light*. In lending it to a friend, or stimulating one to go hunt himself up a copy, one does so also with the pleasant knowledge that one is letting him in for a real aesthetic experience.

Many of the contributors to this symposium have referred to the relationship between Alice Corbin and her husband, William Penhallow Henderson. The creative demonstration of this relationship is in *Brothers of Light*, a work in which the author assumed a different role in many ways from her role in her other published works. There are, first, two forms of fairly obvious collaboration. The observations on the Penitentes were made by the two together, indeed could hardly have been made by a woman alone, since much of Penitente ritual is man's business. There is the collaboration of writer and graphic artist, the one producing the written work, the other contributing, not only illustrations, but a finely worked-out typography and format, so much so that a new edition of this book—which is devoutly to be prayed for—would be incomplete did it not closely reproduce the old.

This second element of collaboration, through which a large-scale publisher was caused to produce such a book as ordinarily comes from the special presses at a very special price, also reflects the fact that the author is indeed a poet, in the technical sense of the word. Your true poet's work is usually a slow distillate. His attitude towards its presentation inevitably differs from that of the prose writer, who produces an infinitely larger volume of writings of assorted lengths and deems his creative years arid indeed if they do not leave him credited with a minimum of a dozen solid books. The prose writer takes a hard-boiled, professional attitude towards the manufacture of the volumes which contain his work; he would never think of harassing his publisher with advice as to format. As for illustrations, all he asks is to be spared them, for not in a thousand seekings will he find one illustrator who will fulfill, rather than destroy, the images he has created. Corbin turned prose writer remained poet.

The existence of this single treatise, this monograph—for the latter term can correctly be applied to it—likewise derives from the poetic element. Corbin set out to write a book on the Southwest. Writers of varied ability, mostly on the modest side, have turned out books on the Southwest, or on New Mexico, with all too little effort. Corbin, approaching her whole as if each part must have the perfection of a poem, has brought only this one section to publishable completion. This one is not comparable to any other writing of similar expressed purpose that I know of. It stands as at once the best thing that has been written about the Penitentes artistically, and as the definitive published work on the subject to date. It is both scholarly and beautiful.

In the applicability of the adjective "scholarly," in the genuine research underlying the literary presentation, we find another aspect of the Corbin-Henderson collaboration, informal and indirect in part, perhaps, direct and overt in part, I know. I do not know how much of the scholar Corbin had in her to start with; not too much I suspect. Henderson had that bent definitely. As an artist, as an architect, as an observer and relisher of the Southwest, he was deeply read, loaded with far-ranging comparisons. I suspect that it was from him that his wife acquired the habit of backing her keen observations, her poet's perceptions, with learning. It is definite that in *Brothers of Light* a goodly part of the comparative material which gives the book much of its scientific weight was originally suggested to her by Henderson. *Brothers of Light* is a book which an anthropologist can read profitably and cite unhesitatingly, not only as to the observations therein recorded, but as to reasoning and evidence on the history of the Penitente pattern. This is due to a collaboration, not just on one book, but in life, the constant exchange of the riches of two minds.

In the 1930's a veteran southwestern ethnologist constantly belabored her colleagues because, in considering the origins of various Indian patterns and rituals, they completely ignored comparable or contrasting practices of old Spain, data which might importantly change their thinking. In 1937 Corbin published *Brothers of Light*, which does not, of course, deal with the Indians, but with a cult vulgarly supposed to be unique to the old Spanish area of New Mexico. Her reasoning concerning its origins and wide relationships is firmly based on comparative studies of Mexico and Spain. There are no footnotes in this book, none of the appanage of science; indeed, the author merely set out to be intelligent and complete. Papal prohibitions of public flagellations may be traced back to 1349, the descent of the Third Order of Saint Francis may be traced, but this is done so smoothly that even the scientific reader is lulled out of recognition that the book is what, were it made a bit more formidable, he would automatically call a "monograph."

When a scientifically minded poet produces a poetical piece of science, all one can do is praise God. The temptation is to search the book for quotations, but in a descriptive work of this kind, quotations of reasonable length are more likely to be demonstrations of inept amputation than of the full effect of the author's prose. Here and there a line stands clear, able to be lifted out: in the discussion of Penitente music, on page 73, the paragraph ends with the flashing, descriptive sentence, "These shrill sounds of religious fervor suddenly lifted above the bare desert have the effect of poising the single soul against space." Most of us would take a page trying to say that.

Fiction and non-fiction, we have had a great deal of "penetrating" or "understanding" writing about the native peoples of the Southwest.

(Respectable writing about Spanish-Americans or Indians by themselves does not exist, from any period, except for certain autobiographies taken down by scientists, and even these are on the esoteric side.) Some writers muscularly lose themselves in an alleged identification with their alien subjects. Some write studies from an Olympian, "we must understand them" point of view. Some, like Mary Austin, create literary images and then describe them, producing reality once removed. One group, outstandingly D. H. Lawrence (one wonders what T. E. might have given us), sets out in a complex search for simplicity, peering through refractions of a mysticism they have brought with them and superimposed upon the country, a sort of prismatic vulva in which they see only their own problems surrounded by rainbows. When this last tendency is combined with neo-Rousseauesque sentimentalism, we reach the impressively adorned abyss of Hiawatha in modern dress.

The writers' fallacies derive from more general ones which we observe in the daily attitudes of what might be called "the reading class," collectors of Indian art, of Spanish *bultos* and folklore. There is the Lord-and-Lady Bountiful approach, how kind we are to these people, and the attitude which asks you to observe them treating the quaint natives as if they really were equals. There is the wildly sentimental. What is extremely rare is the man-to-man relationship, with solid, hard judgment of one's fellow man's weaknesses and strengths, respect both for one's self and for him, the true friendship which wishes to be understood as well as to understand. It is this relationship which the Hendersons established with a great diversity of people, with the entire naturalness of the simple and of true artists. It is none the less genuine for being enlightened with a poet's perceptions and enriched by research. Without it, neither the poems quoted in Mr. Fletcher's article in this symposium nor *Brothers of Light* could have been written.

VI

BROTHERS OF LIGHT
1937 EDITION

BROTHERS OF LIGHT

The Penitentes of the Southwest

BY ALICE CORBIN HENDERSON

ILLUSTRATIONS BY WILLIAM PENHALLOW HENDERSON

ILLUSTRATIONS

"Nuestro Padre Jesus"	*frontispiece*
Cross-Bearers and Flagellants	1
Francisco with Wood from the Mountains	5
Old Morada, El Rito de Santa Fe	11
New Mexican Placita	17
Penitente Morada, Abiquiu	23
Night Procession of the Penitentes	29
La Carreta del Muerto	33
Procesión de Sangre, Good Friday Morning	41
The Crucifixion, Good Friday	47
Visitation of the Sick	59
Penitente Procession, Daytime	69
Old Hacienda, New Mexico	79
Ranchito, Penitente Country	109
"Every House Has Its Door and Its Cross"	119

BROTHERS OF LIGHT

The Penitentes of the Southwest

F one travels through the small villages of northern New Mexico during Holy Week, one is surprised at their unusual quiet and the general absence of men about the place. A few young boys or very old men may be seen, but no able-bodied grown men will be found, either in the fields or the corral, or on the sunny side of the house.

Ask any young woman where her husband or father is, and she will reply casually, "Oh, he has gone up into the mountains to get wood," or "He has gone to find some stray cattle over in the Jemez."

After Holy Week, if you return that way, you may discover that the good man is in bed. "He caught cold up in the mountains," or "He had a fall from his horse." But he will be all right again in a few days, you are told. You are not, however, invited in to see him, as neighbors usually are when there is any sickness in the house; and you also may have noticed, at your first visit, that no horse or burro was missing from the corral during the time when he was supposed to be "up in the mountains." But, being wise, you said nothing. For you knew all the time that he, and all the other men of the village, were at the *Morada*—the adobe chapel of the *Penitente* Brotherhood. And you knew very well why you were not invited into the house; you might see something to make you realize that it was from no fall from a horse or ordinary cold that Francisco was recovering. With tacit understanding, you take your departure, promising to come again when Francisco is better. For you remember certain scenes that you have witnessed.

Imagine as amphitheater a stretch of sun-bleached soil extending from the valley of the Rio Grande to the foothills of the Sangre de Cristo mountains. The river itself is hidden by leafless, silvery-white cottonwoods, and from these the eye ranges across sandy hillocks up to a ridge of red cliffs cutting against blue snow-capped mountains. Over all is the bright clear light of an early spring day; and certainly nothing could be more open and free and remote from mystery than this level stretch of country bared to the candid light of the steadily mounting sun.

Yet suddenly the silence is broken by a thin pin-point of sound—a shrill, unearthly piping, which comes as it were from the air itself. Before we can realize what it means, the near-by ridge is topped by a line of wooden crosses, under which, as the heavy cross-beams reach the crest, we see the staggering figures of black-cowled half-nude men, followed by other men whose naked backs are stained a deep crimson from the blows of the yucca lash with which they are flogging themselves. It

is a wayside procession of the *Hermanos de Luz,* or *Los Hermanos Penitentes,* making one of their yearly Lenten-tide pilgrimages.

At the head of the procession, the *Hermano Mayor,* Chief Brother, carries a life-size crucifix of an emaciated and bleeding Christ. Beside him walks the *Rezador,* or reader, chanting the ritual from a small notebook; and on the other side is the *Pitero,* whose small wooden *pito,* or flute, is producing the shrill notes, punctuated by the wet thud of the lashes, the monotonous rise and fall of a sad Miserere. The responses to this mournful hymn are sung by a straggling line of men in blue jean trousers and black coats, who follow or precede the flagellants.

When the first Spanish conquerors and Franciscan priests came to this country, they brought with them this custom of flagellation as a part of their religious practice; and the Penitent Brotherhood in New Mexico today, although no longer recognized by the Church, is an outgrowth and survival of the Third Order of St. Francis.

As early as 1598, it is recorded that Don Juan de Oñate and his men performed public penance during Holy Week, under the spiritual guidance of the Franciscan friars. Another early reference to the custom of flagellation is found in the chronicle of Fray Alonso de

Benavides, addressed to His Catholic Majesty, Philip IV, in 1630:

"I cannot refrain from telling here a saying of the Demon, by the mouth of an Indian Wizard who was convinced of the word of God, when I began the conversion of the great pueblo of the Xumanas, the which I dedicated to the glorious San Isidoro, Archbishop of Sevilla, because of having begun the conversion on his day.

"And it befell that seeing himself convinced, and that under my reasoning all the pueblo had determined to be Christian, the Wizard was much angered and said at the top of his voice: 'You Spaniards and Christians, how crazy you are! And you live like crazy folks! You want to teach us that we be crazy also!' I asked him wherein we were crazy. And he must have seen some procession of penance during Holy Week in some pueblo of Christians, and so he said: 'You Christians are so crazy that you go all together, flogging yourselves like crazy people in the streets, shedding your blood. And thus you must wish that this pueblo be also crazy!' And with this, greatly angered and yelling [dando voces] he went forth from the pueblo, saying that *he* did not wish to be crazy. Over which matter we were left laughing, and I much more, since I recognized and was persuaded that it was the Demon, who thus went fleeing confounded by the virtue of the Divine Word."

Whether one shares the horror of the Indian Wizard, or the naïve faith of Alonso de Benavides, it is evident from this passage that the Lenten ceremonies of *Los Hermanos de Sangre de Cristo,* or *Los Hermanos de Luz,* as the Brotherhood now variously calls itself, are not the result of contact with savage rites of Indian tribes, as sometimes contended, but represent a genuine Old-World survival.

The Old-World descent is doubly obvious to one who has witnessed the religious processions in Seville during Holy Week. When one hears the thin shrill notes of the *Penitente pito* blown against the New Mexico hills, one remembers instantly the high shrill notes of the silver horn preceding the magnificent *pasos* carried by barefoot penitents through the narrow streets of Seville. Those gorgeous processions, when Seville relives its medieval past—those heavy, life-sized images of martyred Saints, Descents from the Cross, Gardens of Gethsemane, or Virgins resplendent in jewels, are recalled instantly as the true progenitors of the crude *Cristos, Madonnas,* and *Santos* which the humble people of New Mexico carry each year in procession to and from the local Calvary, performing in the meanwhile such penance as was the custom in the Middle Ages throughout all Europe. And even the crude death-cart, the *Carreta del Muerto* of the *Penitente* processions—is not its spirit precisely that of those old Moralities, Dances of Death, the paintings and prints (like Dürer's "The Knight, Death, and the Devil"), in which the macabre religious emotion of the Middle Ages expressed itself?

That these Old-World customs have persisted in New Mexico is due in part to the extreme isolation of the people, in what was the northernmost fringe of Spanish empire in the New World. And this isolation was further emphasized shortly after the Mexican revolution, when the Spanish-born Franciscans were expelled from the country, and the native people were left to perform their own rituals for weddings or christenings or funerals. What more natural then, than that this Order of the laity should assume the rôle and duty of the priesthood, and be loath to relinquish it entirely when the secular priests returned? Even today the New Mexico parishes include a wide sweep of rough country and many villages. The resident priest in one of the villages visits the others in rotation. Often in bad weather, when roads are impassable, the priest cannot reach the bedside of one who is sick or dying. Then it is that the *Hermanos* pray and keep vigil beside the sick person, and administer help and comfort to the family. Thus

the Brotherhood is really active throughout the year, although it is only during Lent that the entire Brotherhood takes part in public penance.

The belief in the efficacy of this self-imposed penance is of course deeply devout—it is the old doctrine of suffering as an atonement for sin; and it is this sincere faith which makes the *Penitente* ceremonies so moving.

Usually spring comes late in northern New Mexico, and if Easter falls early, the *Penitentes* may make their pilgrimages through snow or sleet. Again, when Easter comes in April, apricot and peach trees shed a drift of petals across the roads, the soft charm of the valleys contrasting with the sharp edges of red sandstone cliffs and blue mountain peaks still topped with snow. In this landscape of strange and austere beauty, the processions of the *Penitentes* have a significance of form and color which enhances the undeniably mystic element of their ceremonies. The heavy massed wooden crosses against the sky; the half-nude, barefooted men staggering under the weight of the heavy cross-beams; the upraised arms of the flagellants, as with a regular monotonous rhythm, they bring the braided yucca whip first over one shoulder and then the other; the crude blindfolded *Cristo* in red dress, with black hair streaming in the wind; the heavy tired faces of the accompanying *Hermanos*; the old women in black shawls with but the V-shaped white of the face showing, looking exactly like the death-figure on the *Carreta del Muerto*—all this has an inescapable emotional effect upon us, even though the faith that is moving these simple, impassioned people out of a bygone century is buried deep down in some remote fiber of our own race-memory.

N New Mexico, the farther you go from railroads and highways, the farther back in time you find yourself. A wagon-road or a trail to a small mountain village may lead you into the Seventeenth Century, so little have customs and manner of living changed. And when the customs are traditional, as in religious ceremonies, the atmosphere is that of an even earlier century. This is as true today—in spite of the easier access by new roads—as it was several years ago when we traveled sixty-five long arduous miles from Santa Fe to spend Holy Week in a small village on the Chama River. About twenty-five miles above San Juan, where the Chama River flows into the Rio Grande, Abiquiu sits on a shelf below the Jemez mountains, facing, over the river valley below, the far distant slopes of the *Sangre de Cristo* range. On the left of the village, a

great copper-colored cliff juts into the valley, making a bend in the river. Sheltered from the west by the Jemez, on the south by a volcanic ridge, and on the north by the copper cliffs, the valley is well-watered and fertile. Flowering fruit trees in spring, and pale, branching, unleafed cottonwoods make a thread of silver and pink against the red earth of the river bed and the equally red-colored houses in the valley. Abiquiu itself is more bare and austere. Its brown earth houses, with tiny white-washed courtyards, are clustered about a bare plaza, swept and empty, except for a few low adobes on one side of the middle space and on the other a large cross standing in front of the church. Facing us, as we drove into the village, was the trading-post of our destination, on the opposite side of the plaza—a two-story frame building, set in an orchard, with a long, low porch in front and gabled windows in the upper story.

We had left Santa Fe in the morning, but it was late afternoon before we reached Abiquiu. Travel by car in those early days involved all the hazards of a steeplechase. The last twenty-five miles was mostly a two-rut wagon road, with deep sandy stretches, or caving banks, spanned by wooden bridges—almost invariably washed out. On the way up the valley, it had commenced to drizzle, and as we entered Abiquiu, a light rain was falling. The car made the last steep grade with a slippery groan, and, if we had hoped to steal in unnoticed under the *Morada,* which stands on top of the hill, our wish would have been futile. But, fortunately, we had no such wish, or fear; our coming, as invited guests, was expected; and as our car with a last groan and skid, made the crest, we were greeted by the son of our host, who stepped on the running-board.

Our first question was prompted, naturally, by curiosity.

"Is anything happening?"

"Yes, plenty. The *Hermano Mayor* says it is all right and he is very glad to have you come. Only you must not go too near the *Morada* or the processions. I was looking out for you on the hill just now and did not notice I was going so near the *Morada*—they came out and shoo'ed me off; one of the boys threw a stone at me, but I think it was because he wanted to—I always beat him at baseball."

Jo had been born in Abiquiu, but he had been away at school in the East and had only recently come back to help his father in the trading-store. "You needn't mind," Jo said, "if my father seems quiet. He's been here so long and seen so few people except natives and Indians, that he has got out of the habit of talking."

Jo took us upstairs to our bedrooms with the gabled

windows, where a tall Navajo woman was spreading bright-colored Chimayo blankets on our beds. Jo introduced her to us as his nurse, "Schone," an abbreviation of her Spanish name, *Encarnación*. She had taken care of him and of his older brothers and sisters, from the time they were born. When he repeated this in Spanish for her benefit, her withered brown face crinkled into a smile. Jo told us what he knew of her history; that she had been brought to Abiquiu as a child, perhaps as a captive after a raid on the Navajos. Now she was keeping house for his father while the rest of the family were away. Jo's elder brother was then a secretary of the American Legation in Madrid.

Abiquiu in the early days, like Taos on the north, was exposed to frequent attacks of Utes, Navajos, and other Apaches. Originally established by the Spaniards as a *Genízaro* pueblo, it was wiped out of existence by the Utes in 1747; and later resettled with an increased Spanish population. None of the *Genízaro* pueblos remained long as such. Like Tomé or Belen in the south, Abiquiu soon became almost entirely Spanish. What admixture of Indian blood remained was submerged in the dominating Spanish strain, as seems almost invariably the case in a union of these two races. Today in Abiquiu, pure Spanish descent is traced by several families of the old Grandee or Don class; and the facial type, as we came to realize during the ceremonies, is predominantly Spanish. Many of the men could easily have stepped out of an El Greco or early Velasquez painting.

While we stood there talking, Jo pulled aside the curtain of the south window and showed us, over the apple orchard, a high stretch of bare ground against a black buttress of volcanic rock. This, he said, was where the *Penitente* processions passed from the lower *Morada* to the upper *Morada* beyond. Between the two was the *Campo Santo,* used as a symbolic Calvary for processions from both *Moradas.* We were just about to turn away when Jo said suddenly, "Here they come now!" and we caught a glimpse, over the tree-tops, of a single barefoot *penitente*, walking slowly in the direction of the *Campo Santo*. His head was shrouded in a black hood, and his arms were folded across his breast. Several men in ordinary clothes walked beside him. The sight of the black-hooded, emaciated figure in the misty rain, with the plaintive notes of the *pito,* blowing in over the blossom-scented air, had an indescribably eerie effect.

A fold of land hid the small procession from view, and we hurried downstairs, through the flowering trees and over a low stone wall, to overtake it. We could still hear the shrill *pito* in the field above, as we climbed breathlessly up to the level space; and we reached the top just as the small procession had turned into the path leading to the *Campo Santo.*

We followed as closely as we dared, and found that the group consisted of the penitent, with a *Compañero* on either side, the flute-player, and the *Hermano Mayor,* carrying a small black cross with a silver figure of Christ Crucified upon it. But our attention was immediately riveted upon the penitent. A branch of forked rattlesnake cactus was tightly bound by a rope to his naked back and chest, and over the cactus his arms were folded across his breast. From the stiff, extended fingers of one hand dangled a rosary. His legs, clad in thin cotton drawers rolled up to the knees, were each tightly wound with a horse-hair rope all the way down to the ankles.

At the gate, there was a momentary cessation of the wailing notes of the *pito,* while all fell upon their knees, and the *Hermano Mayor* recited a brief prayer. Then the leaders rose, and all followed the penitent, who, still upon his knees, crept slowly up to the large cross in the center of the enclosure. At a grave in one corner, an old woman in a black shawl was kneeling. She did not cease to kneel, nor did she turn her head to notice the penitents at any time while they remained in the cemetery. About halfway up to the cross, the penitent began to move even more slowly and painfully, for a path of cactus was strewn over the ground, and over this he inched slowly along on his knees up to the cross. At its foot, he bent his head to kiss the cross, then extended himself full length, face down, with his arms still folded over the cactus. The other Brothers knelt beside him, and after a certain number of prayers had been said, the penitent rose again to a kneeling position and, still on his knees, with his face to the cross, moved slowly backwards, inch by inch, to the gate. Here he was helped to his feet, and the group turned back toward the *Morada*. The faces of the men, as they passed us, were stoic, immobile, absorbed in the rite.

The *Morada* would have been indistinguishable from any other adobe house, but for the heavy crosses piled up outside it, a single upright cross planted before the door, and the one small window placed high up in the wall. As we sat watching the small group take the last steps, the door of the *Morada* was opened, to close upon the penitent and his companions; and we were left with the sound of the *pito* and the harsh droning voices still ringing in our ears.

As we took a round-about way back through the plaza, Jo showed us a dark stain on the mud wall of a house where a penitent had stood and lashed himself

until he couldn't lift another stroke of the whip. "In fulfillment of a vow," Jo said.

When we came out from supper, Jo was in the little wire-screened office sorting the mail. The store was dimly lit by kerosene lamps. Ambrosio, Schone's nephew, was waiting on customers, and a few straggling children were buying the usual penny's worth of this and that. One man bought a pair of *calzones*, the white cotton drawers worn by the *Penitentes*. He rolled them up, unwrapped, and stuck them in his pocket. He, and several other men who came in, had a strained look about the eyes—as if stretched open by an effort of will against sleepiness.

We asked Ambrosio, who was part Indian and not a *Penitente*, if he thought there would be a Crucifixion. He lifted his shoulders and said *"Quien sabe?"* There had always been one, and why not this year?

While we were waiting for Jo, we strolled outside into the plaza, and seeing a light in the church, we walked up to the open door and looked in. There were no pews in the church, only a few wooden benches in front of the altar, and back of these on the hard earth floor stood a line of small and large *Santos*—the native wooden images of the saints—lit by tall candles burning before them and dripping pools of melted tallow at their feet.

Facing the *Santos,* with their backs toward us, was a row of conical black shapes—kneeling women in black shawls; among them one girl, whose shawl had slipped off, knelt with her forehead to the ground before one of the images, in complete self-forgetful devotion.

In the light of the candles, the crudely carved faces of the saints were curiously real and living. The largest of the figures, a *Cristo,* was clothed in a long red garment, with hands tied before him, eyes blindfolded with a white cloth, and a crown of thorns on his long black hair. An image of *San José* was clothed in white, and *San Pedro* and several other saints of smaller size wore silk dresses and hats of a bygone style. All of the figures, except one, were of native craft, the primitive wood sculpture of this country, in which passion and beauty are instinctively chiseled in the crudely painted wooden features. Only one of the figures—a small blue and white image of the Virgin—was obviously a store product, with a marked resemblance to Queen Victoria, looking queerly out of place among the genuine expressions of native genius.

In the early days, much of the ecclesiastical art was brought to this country from Old Mexico or from Spain. But as this was replaced by the work of native craftsmen, the local hierarchy of saints and archangels began to look, not like the people of Renaissance Italy, but like the native people of mountainous and arid New Mexico. The austerity of Spain was retained in the blood be-spattered *Cristos* (like those of the Spanish sculptor Montañes), with touches of Indian paganism in the Astarte-eyed Virgins of Guadalupe. This crude, direct realism bothered the later French priests who came to New Mexico with Archbishop Lamy in 1851, and this is said to be the reason why the people began to cover their painted saints with dresses and bonnets. But more probably it was prompted by that instinct of simple devotion which gives to the Saints all that the people themselves desire to possess.

As these spare figures of black-bearded Saints reflect the features of the people, so too do they reflect the native life and landscape. If the features are harsh and the creed of the people is harsh, so too is the soil. The life of the people, wrung from an arid soil dependent upon wind and chance, is overcast by a somber fatalism. The reach of the peaks and the stretch of the plateaus overshadow one's small life; yet life lifts itself against them to sing its small song—and vanish.

Something of all this we felt as we stood there: in the mood of the kneeling women and the girl bent half-prostrate before the Saints—Saints not of Italy or of Jerusalem, but of the bare red earth of New Mexico.

The moon by this time was breaking through a

cloudy sky; we should not have clear moonlight, nor, on the other hand, complete darkness. We had been hearing for some time the whirring noise of the *metraca*, as a signal to the members of the Brotherhood to assemble, and we now caught the inevitable sound of the *pito* coming nearer.

Hurrying to find a place where we could see the procession coming down from the *Morada*, we took a wrong turn and found ourselves caught in a passageway between two houses which led, not to the road, but to a small patio with a single lighted window. While we stood there, uncertain which way to go, we heard sounds coming from inside the room with the lighted window. It was a subdued wailing, first low and then becoming more shrill. Women's voices, crying, "*Mi hermano, mi hermano!*"—my brother, my brother! A cloth was pinned across the lower sash of the window, but above this, by standing on tiptoe, we could see into the room. In one corner a man, heavily bandaged, was lying in bed, and around the room sat wailing women completely muffled in black shawls.

Outside, on the other side of the house, we could hear the crunch of dragging crosses and the sound of the *pito* coming nearer. Suddenly these noises ceased, the door of the room opened, and several *Penitentes* entered. The leaders carried small black crucifixes and rosaries; the

cross-bearers, having left their crosses outside, entered on their knees, with their black-cowled heads bowed, and hands crossed over their breasts. The wailing of the women broke into a shrill keen, while the leading *Hermanos* said prayers over the sick man. The low recitative prayers and responses, accompanied by softened notes from the *pito,* ended with a chant. Then all withdrew, except the women, two of whom threw themselves across the foot of the bed, in an agony of grief.

Finding our way back to the plaza, we stood in the shadow of one of the low adobe buildings, where we could watch the procession passing. It was now quite dark, except for half moonlight in a mottled sky. The bulk of the church loomed against the edge of the copper cliff, and the light from the church streamed through the open door upon the large cross in the plaza. As the *Penitentes* came nearer, the people in the church, now joined by many other men, women, and children, came out from the church and stood on one side of the cross facing the procession of penitents. The *Hermano Mayor* with a small crucifix, the *Rezador* carrying the small handwritten copy-book of the ritual, and the *Pitero* with his flute led the procession. These were followed by five cross-bearers, each with a *Compañero,* on either side. The long heavy beam rested on the shoulder of each bearer, the cross-arm projecting vertically upward, and the end of the heavy main timber dragged crunchingly over the ground. Each *Compañero* carried a lantern on his outer side, throwing crossed bars of light and shadow over the procession. The *Rezador* carried his lantern locked in one arm, with its light falling on the pages of his small copy-book.

Following the cross-bearers came a penitent dragging the *Carreta del Muerto*. This was a very heavy low wooden cart, with solid wooden wheels, like the old ox-carts. On it sat a small figure of Death, clothed in a rusty black dress, with staring obsidian eyes in a chalk-white face. The eyes caught whatever glint of light fell upon them, even though the face was in shadow, giving to the dead mask an uncanny sense of life. The figure held a drawn bow with the arrow stretched for flight. Tradition has it that the arrow once left the bow to strike the heart of a mocking bystander, killing him instantly. Variations of this tradition exist through all the mountain villages and are occasionally applied to some specific person, long since dead.

Sometimes the figure on the cart is blindfolded, indicating death's blind uncertainty. Also other primitive instruments of death are sometimes concealed in the cart—an ax-head, a stone hammer, or a heavy rock.

The figure of death is in reality a carefully carved skeleton: and some of these figures are very finely

conceived, with beautiful articulation of form.

The penitent dragged the *Carreta del Muerto* by a horse-hair rope passed over his shoulders and under his arm-pits, the painful weight of the dragging cart cutting into his naked flesh—a penance as severe as any other, and increased by the fact that the axles of the cart were stationary, and where there was a turn in the path, the entire cart and its inflexible wheels were dragged by main strength.

Several flagellants followed the *Carreta*. The rhythmic stroke of the yucca lash came down with a wet swish and thud on their dripping backs, the heavy lash lifted with both hands and swung first over one shoulder and then the other; then a few steps taken, and another stroke of the lash. Not—in spite of the spectacular sight of blood—so severe a penance as some others. The next single penitent was a man of extraordinarily powerful build, his entire torso tightly bound with branching cactus, the rope tightly bound also about each leg, and his ankles shackled with heavy dragging iron chains. This was a much stronger and younger man than the cactus-bound penitent of the afternoon; but he was evidently deeply moved, quite apart from the physical strain of the ordeal; for he was sobbing in the folds of his black silk hood—sobbing and repeating the refrain of the hymn all were singing:

Penitencia, penitencia,
Ya no peques, hombre atros,
Examina tu conciencia,
Ven al templo oye la voz.

Tiempo es de hacer penitencia,
Hombre que estas divertido
Al no haber te arrepentido
Examina tu conciencia.

Penitence, penitence,
Sin no more, unfortunate man,
Examine your conscience,
Come to the temple and hear the Voice.

It is time to make penance,
You who have been too busy
To take warning to repent,
Examine your conscience.

When the leaders of the procession reached the cross in front of the church, they stopped to meet the people coming out of the door, bearing the images of Jesus and the Virgin Mary—the Virgin in white, and Christ in crimson. The two groups stood facing each other until, at a signal from the *Hermano Mayor,* followed by a whirl of the *Metraca,* the entire procession halted and knelt in the road.

At this point, one companion of each of the cross-bearers stooped, with hands over his head, to lift the cross from the shoulders of the bearer, and then stood so supporting it, with hands over his head (another penance), while the cross-bearers knelt before the large cross and kissed its foot. Then, under the shadow of their own crosses, they lay face downward with arms outstretched, making of themselves another sign of the cross. The men with the lanterns held them in such a way as to screen the penitents in shadow. Not entirely, however, could this be done. In the half moonlight and half lantern-light, under the alternate bars of light and shadow, the long line of kneeling or prostrate penitents, all momentarily hushed in the subdued chanting, made a powerfully dramatic impression. The clock of time had mysteriously turned back. This was not the United States or the Twentieth Century, but the heart of the Middle Ages.

Again, at a whirring signal from the *Metraca,* the procession commenced to move. The leaders, accompanied by the people carrying the images of Christ and the Virgin, began to circle the Plaza, stopping at intervals as each group of penitents reached the Cross and prostrated themselves before it. When it came his turn, the swarthy cactus-bound penitent, laid prone upon his thorny cuirass, gave way to convulsive weeping, while sweat poured from his body. *"Pecado—pecado!"* "I have sinned—I have sinned!"

This, on Wednesday of Holy Week, was our initiation—vicarious—into the rites of the *Penitentes*. Our further initiation, during the two following days, was such that we felt afterward that no physical participation could have left us more saturated in their spirit.

That night we witnessed seemingly endless processions that followed one another, first from one *Morada* and then the other, to and from the cross in the plaza and back again. The cumulative impression cast a spell obliterating all sense of the age in which we were living. When we went to bed finally the processions had stopped. Outside our window, as we fell asleep, we still heard the slap of whips, the crunch of dragging crosses, the squeaking wheels of the *Carreta,* and the shrill notes of the *pito* mingling with the tired huskiness of chanting voices.

The next day, Holy Thursday, was very largely a repetition of smaller processions of flagellants, crossbearers, or individual penitents, all day long—including pilgrimages to far-off shrines in the hills, or to a chapel hidden in a cluster of houses in the valley. In the afternoon, the people in the village recited the Stations of the Cross in the church. At night the processions in the plaza were repeated. We watched; and were again immersed in the spirit of past centuries.

HEN we waked on Good Friday morning, it was with a pleasant sense of light and warmth. The sun was shining with full April strength, and birds were singing in the orchard beneath our window. But it was only a moment before we recalled that we must get up quickly if we were not to miss the early morning procession. In fact, when we reached the field above the orchard, we found that we were just in time. Thirty-seven flagellants were in line, coming out from the *Campo Santo*, whipping themselves vigorously in rhythmic unison. It was a repetition of black-cowled heads, bare bodies, white cotton drawers, and bright red splashes on backs and trousers. This was the celebrated *Procession de Sangre* of Good Friday morning. With it were no *Compañeros*, or *pito*-player or *Rezador*—only the thirty-seven men steadily flogging themselves. As the procession moved toward the place where we stood, one of the flagellants left the line and came towards us, still stopping at each step or two to lift his hands and

give himself a stroke of the whip. For a moment, we had a panicky fear that he was intending to include us in the penance! Then it occurred to us that he might suspect us of having a camera, and we spread our empty hands wide apart to reassure him. Evidently this had been his thought, and with a wave of his whip to motion us farther back, he regained his place in the line.

The procession, moving quickly, went into the lower *Morada;* and, after a little while, about half the number, still whipping vigorously, returned to the upper *Morada.*

After breakfast, we spent a pleasant hour loafing in the orchard. It was good, after our excursion in Time of the past two days, to feel ourselves in our own skins again, with the sun on our backs, and those backs whole and unbroken! Occasionally we wandered up on the hill to watch the various small processions. There were not quite so many of these as on the day before; but we found another interest in the groups of visitors from other villages who began to appear. From our chairs in the orchard we had a glimpse of the plaza, and could watch the people passing.

A certain holiday spirit, subdued by a hushed solemnity, pervaded the village. Young boys and girls were clothed in Sunday finery; the boys in bright blue suits and black sombreros; the girls in high-heeled shoes, silk

dresses, and elaborate hats, under which their dark faces, covered with white powder, acquired an extraordinary lavender tinge. These young people belonged to the Twentieth Century. But the older women of the generation passing wore their black shawls and went, first of all, into the church to pray. A few wagons drove into the plaza and tied at the hitching rail in front of the store. The wagons had chairs or benches to accommodate the entire family, from grandmothers to babies in arms. Colored Chimayo blankets were spread on the backs of the seats and over the knees, to protect their clothes from the dust. Soon the plaza and the field above presented a gala appearance, very different from the day before, when we had been the sole audience. Prevailing over all, was an air of expectancy; but we were told that the Crucifixion never took place before the afternoon.

The principal procession before noon was led by a barefoot penitent, in the usual black cowl, and bloodstained white drawers, carrying a tall blindfolded *Cristo* in a red dress—the black hair streaming out in the wind. After this, garish in the full daylight, came the figure of Death on the *Carreta del Muerto,* dragged by a penitent in the same blood-stained costume, with one man beside him singing hymns, and another one holding a rope tied to the back of the cart to prevent its going downhill too fast. Next, a penitent with cactus bound over breast and back, and chains from the ankles; then five cross-bearers, each with a companion, the last *Compañero* lustily singing responses to the stanzas of the *Rezador,* who walked in front beside the *Carreta.*

This procession was followed by all the black-shawled women, boys, men, and girls from the neighboring villages, who crowded into the small chapel of the *Morada,* where the image of Christ was carried. Those who could not get into the room knelt on the ground outside the open door, through which floated the sound of chanted prayers and hymns.

High noon now stood over the valley—the time when in all parish churches the Three Hours' services begin, commemorating Christ's agony and death on the Cross. But in this, as in other small Mexican communities, where there are no resident priests, the Penitent Brotherhood has its own way of observing the ritual of Christ's death.

The services in the *Morada* were comparatively short, and it was not long before the entire village seemed deserted, the visitors having gone into the houses of their friends to rest. We, too, after lunch, enjoyed a brief siesta, then wandered up on the hillside where, by that time, everyone was waiting.

"Is it true," we again asked Schone's nephew, "is

there really going to be a Crucifixion?" And he again answered, "*Sí, seguro. Porqué no?*" "Yes, certainly. Why not?" So we sat on a low stone wall, just below the *Morada*, and waited. All the other people were waiting, too; sitting quietly like ourselves, or moving about and talking. Boys and girls strolled about together in awkward self-consciousness. One could see by the lifted eyebrows of some of the older women that they thought little of this new freedom, with its lack of that strict chaperonage formerly insisted upon in this, as in all Spanish countries.

The *Morada* meanwhile gave no sign of life, save for a thin line of smoke going up from the chimney and, in watching the people on this hillside, we had almost forgotten the object of our waiting, when, without any preamble whatsoever, a man came out the door of the *Morada* and commenced to dig a small deep hole a little way in front of the house. The whole hillside became hushed at once, and everyone crowded along the stone wall.

Another man came out of the *Morada* to help the first, and the two tested the depth of the hole by setting up in it one of the wooden crosses which were stacked up in front of the *Morada*. Evidently the hole was not deep enough, so after more digging it was tested again —this time with a heavier and very much bigger cross, evidently to their satisfaction, for the cross was then taken down and carried into the *Morada*. For some time nothing happened. Then, finally, a group of men came out carrying a small wooden platform on which stood the almost life-sized *Cristo* in a red dress. Again the door opened, and the heavy cross, with a living man bound upon it, was carried out, with its cross-beam upward, through the door and laid upon the ground with its foot on the edge of the hole made ready to receive it. Slowly and carefully the cross was raised into place, turned facing the *Morada*, and made firm; and on the cross hung the supreme penitent, in imitation of his Saviour. Facing the penitent on the cross stood the red-robed *Cristo*, who, with eyes no longer blindfolded, thus acknowledged His living disciple. At the foot of the cross, the *Hermano Mayor* and other leaders of the Brotherhood knelt praying. The black-cowled figure on the cross wore only the white cotton drawers rolled up as a loin-cloth. His wrists and arms were bound to the main timber by a horse-hair rope. Around his chest, a band of linen supplemented the rope, and eased the strain somewhat.

For ten, fifteen, seventeen minutes—and they seemed ages long as we waited—the figure hung on the cross; then the black-cowled head suddenly fell forward, the body slumped, and the men slowly lowered the cross

and carried it into the *Morada* with the limp figure hanging upon it. The men with the *Cristo* followed singing and the door closed upon them.

Meanwhile, the sun sinking at our backs had turned the cliffs across the valley into splendid cathedral shapes of rose and saffron beauty—a beauty that is touched here in this country with a sometimes terrible sense of eternity, loneliness, and futility. For all the gay laughter of youth on the hillside, the stark parable of the Crucifixion is close to the country's soul. It eats into the heart, this terror; and it is not difficult to imagine how the early Franciscans felt, as they gazed upon this terrible afternoon light on bare mesa and peak, and felt the thorns of this eternal loneliness pressing into their souls. Actual mortification of the flesh is perhaps less poignant. What, one wondered, in such a stark primeval landscape, could call for an artificial terror—for a theatrically induced tragic sense of life and death? Yet we were to have this too, presently, in the symbolic *Tinieblas*.

The night of Good Friday began as on the day before, with lantern-lit pilgrimages from the *Moradas* to the cross in the plaza. Soon we saw a number of people from the village following one of the processions, and Francisca, a young Mexican girl who lived with Schone, came and put her hand in mine and said she would take us to the *Tinieblas* in the upper *Morada* on the hill. She wore a black shawl, and I was glad that she kept close to me lest I should lose her among all the other black-shawled women who were taking the same path.

Going up the road we passed a group of flagellants and cross-bearers coming down, and when we reached the top of the hill we met a similar procession coming around from the direction of the lower *Morada*. These flagellants passed through a door into the secret room; the crosses were taken from the shoulders of their bearers and piled up against the end of the house. As they went in, the light fell full upon the ghastly white face of the Death-image seated outside upon the rude wooden cart.

Francisca took us into the larger room of the *Morada*, which serves as a chapel. Black-shawled women and small children were seated on the floor on the left, and men and boys crowded the floor space on the right-hand side of the room. This division of men and women as regards seating in the churches follows old Spanish custom. They had been having a *Velorio*, or song service, before we went in, and were still singing the last verses of a long narrative hymn which recounts the whole history of Christ's trial and crucifixion. One of the *Hermanos* led the service out of his small copy-book. Those who knew the words joined in the stanzas, and the others, particularly the children, came in lustily on the refrain; which in English would be:

>And the ungrateful people shouted,
>"Let him be crucified!"

At the end of the hymn, the *Rezador* left his place in front of the altar, and went to join the other *Hermanos* who had gone into the back room.

We were seated facing the altar in the slightly curved end of the room. The little chapel was freshly whitewashed, and spotlessly neat. The altar was draped with lace curtains and Chimayo blankets. Candles burned before a small image of the Virgin and Child upon the altar, and a number of larger images were grouped about it. One was a pallid *Cristo,* with a drooping thorn-crowned head, a spear projecting from a wound in one side, and a small wasp-like dove from the other. In front of the altar stood a tall candelabrum, with thirteen candles in the sockets.

The *Hermano* who had led the hymns now came back and said that those who wished to leave before the *Tinieblas* should do so now, as after the doors and windows were shut and the services began, no one would be permitted to do so. He said that there was nothing to be afraid of, but that one must not on any account strike a match or make a light. No one of course left, and the room was now completely crowded. Other brothers meanwhile came in with Navajo blankets which they hung across the one window, covering up every possible crack and crevice. Others brought in heavy iron chains and threw them down on the floor with a clanking noise. The *Rezador* and the *Pitero* came in with a lantern and a large Navajo blanket, and taking up a place in the corner beside the altar, completely wrapped themselves in the blanket, with lantern, hymnbook, and flute, shrouding themselves in what must have been a kerosene-heated sweat-bath. The room was already beginning to grow uncomfortably hot and stuffy.

Francisca and I were seated about the middle of the room, among the closely packed women and children. Just back of us was a very pretty girl whose father was one of the leading men in the village, and, as Francisca whispered to me, a *"Penitente muy importante"*—an important Penitente. Between us and the door into the back room, a space has now cleared, and in this space four flagellants came and knelt, whips in hand. I started to turn around and look at them, but a touch from Francisca warned me not to. The flagellants threw their whips around their shoulders, to see if there was room enough, and I felt Francisca shudder. The ceremony still held its terror for her. There was a growing feeling of fear and suspense. The men who were waiting outside the house were now told to come in; the outer door was closed; the light in the inner room put out—we could hear the other penitents in the inner room crowding as close to its door as possible. Then two of the leading *Hermanos* came in and took their places on either side of the candelabrum, while a third brother, the *Hermano Mayor,* stood near it in front of the altar.

The only light now in the room came from the thirteen candles on the candelabrum. With a signal for silence, the *Hermano Mayor* now commenced the ritual of the service. At the end of each passage, the two brothers beside the candelabrum each pinched out the light of a candle. Gaunt and hollow-eyed from long vigils and lack of sleep, the faces of the three men were typically Spanish in fanatic endurance, with the drawn ascetic features of the martyrs painted by El Greco.

As the number of lighted candles grew fewer, the suspense increased; six, four, two, *one*—then suddenly darkness and pandemonium. Shrieks, sobs, and howls, *metracas* rattling, chains clanking, the *pito* wailing; and through it all the swish, slap, swish, slap of the flagellants' whips just behind us. This was the *Tinieblas,* the shadow, the earthquake—when the heavens were darkened and the earth gaped, and graves were burst asunder. This, too, was Purgatory; and these were the cries of the souls in torment, for whom prayers must be said.

Francisca kept tight hold of my hand, and looking down once at my hand that held hers, I was startled and jumped suddenly at the sight of a tiny light in the pitch darkness—the phosphorescent face of my wrist-watch! It was not then the tiny Hell-flame of my imagination! . . . In addition to the deafening noise, it was suffocating in the tightly closed, packed room. I thought of the two men with the lit lantern under their Navajo blanket; but they probably had emerged from its folds by now: the flute-player at any rate must have, for his *pito* was shrill above the tumult. It was a grateful lull, when, every now and then, the *Hermano Mayor* raised his voice above the hubbub, and commanded *"un Sudario"*—a prayer—for the souls of the dead, for those in Purgatory, for men at war. The Ave Maria at the close of each prayer was a signal for more tumult to begin. Then another prayer; then more tumult. . . .

During one lull, the young girl back of us caused an interruption by complaining bitterly to one of the *Hermanos* near her that "One of those *sal Penitentes* is splashing blood on me!" This caused even Francisca to giggle. The *Hermano* spoke to the flagellants and tried to move them a little farther back. Francisca whispered to me that the *Penitente* was doing it on purpose—he was in love with her, but she didn't like him. Nothing was thought of the interruption, and the ritual went on as before.

I lost track of the number of prayers given. The racket after each intermission was more deafening than before. It seemed ages long before the final Ave Maria was said—final because it was accompanied by the spurt of a match in the hands of the *Hermano Mayor*. The candles upon the altar and in the tin sconces on the walls were lit, and the door opened, with a welcome rush of fresh air.

But before we could arise from our cramped positions, the *Hermano Mayor* raised his hand, and delivered a short address. It was in Spanish, but intended for *los Americanos* present. His words had a simple dignity which commanded respect. We were not to think, he said, that they worshiped—pointing to the images on the altar—these *Muñecas*, these dolls, for themselves. They were the images of the Saints in Heaven; and the ceremonies which we had seen tonight and during the past few days were not savage or barbaric, but were deeply religious mysteries which had been handed down to them by their forefathers from France and Spain. He begged that we would not go away and spread false reports of what we had seen, and what they had permitted us to see. He thanked us for coming, and hoped we would come again, if we wished to. It was a speech of gentle courtesy, to which we responded the next morning, when, before leaving, we paid a call upon him.

The air felt positively cold when we stepped outside. The sky, frosted with stars, seemed blissfully quiet. Walking down the hill, we heard the sound of the inevitable *pito* leading more processions in the plaza; but we thought that the *Tinieblas* was a fitting close to our cumulative impressions.

OS *Hermanos Penitentes de la Tercer Orden de San Francisco* is the name by which the penitent brotherhood in New Mexico was formerly known. Local variants now are *Los Hermanos de Luz,* or *Los Hermanos de Sangre de Cristo,* or simply *Los Hermanos Penitentes.*

The Brotherhood is active not only during Lent, but at stated times throughout the year. Ceremonies take place on certain Saints' days; particularly on those of the patronal Saints of the Third Order of Saint Francis. Also, when a member dies, the *Hermanos* take charge of the three days' *Velorio*, or wake, preceding burial. Flagellation is sometimes a feature of these services.

The Lenten penance begins on Ash Wednesday, and continues throughout Lent, on certain days of each week, culminating in the public penances of Holy Week and the final crucifixion.

We had been told, and one is still told, that the final penance of the crucifixion is a thing of the past. In some communities, the living penitent on the cross is said to be replaced by an image, or by a stuffed figure, so completely shrouded by a sheet that it might be hard to tell if the figure were living or not. It is also said that in earlier times the living penitent was not bound by ropes, but nailed to the cross; but there is no actual evidence of this fact. Deaths from the present form of crucifixion are said to have occurred, but might equally well have resulted from the exhausting strain and exposure of preceding penance. The strain of the crucifixion we witnessed was chiefly that of constriction from the ropes, causing the penitent to faint, at which time the cross was immediately taken down with its limp burden and carried into the *Morada*.

Another story, often told, is that when a *Penitente* dies as the result of penance, away from home, his shoes are sent to his family—this being the only news they receive of his death. This may be a bit of legendary fiction. The Brotherhood, in spite of its morbid absorption in the darker side of life, and in death as its overshadowing aspect—typically Spanish in that!—is essentially a charitable organization, although less is heard of this aspect than of the more spectacular phases of its activities. It is the special duty of one officer to visit the sick and poor, and give comfort and help to the family. The Brotherhood has funds, and, for this purpose, sometimes even maintains its own flock of sheep or goats. An early New Mexican archive records a case of theft from a flock belonging to a *Cofradía*, with due punishment of the offender.

In spite of lurid reports of cruelties administered to lagging penitents by other members of the Brotherhood, nothing seen today indicates anything of this kind; on the contrary, great care is taken by the leading *Hermanos* that the self-imposed penances do not exceed the bounds of human endurance.

Early eye-witnesses tell of lagging penitents or stumbling cross-bearers being whipped to their feet, as examples of deliberate cruelty. But this may have been, rather, a symbolic representation of the scourging before Pilate and of the Three Falls of Christ under His Cross on the way to Calvary. The whole ritual of the Holy Week ceremonies is a replica of Christ's agony—

His trial, suffering, and Crucifixion—each detail of which is dramatized as closely as possible.

It is said that the Penitent Brotherhood only came into prominence in the early half of the Nineteenth Century; but this does not mean that it only then came into existence. Its notoriety at that time was gained through the accounts of early pioneer Americans, notably Gregg and Davis, who, being Protestants, were unused to, and so offended by, any form of religious display. Their condemnation of the *Penitentes* was not more severe than their expressed disapproval of the regular Church processions witnessed in Santa Fe on Good Friday, featuring "life-sized images of Christ and the Virgin, Mary Magdalene and several others, accompanied by the most notorious personages of antiquity, centurions and guards, bestriding splendidly caparisoned horses, in the breathing reality of flesh and blood." In reading accounts of the *Penitentes,* due allowance must be made for the background of the narrator!

Another example of deliberate cruelty often cited is that of the incisions made down the penitent's back with a sharp piece of flint or obsidian, preceding flagellation. But this is for the purpose of allowing the blood to flow freely—less painful than if welts were raised—and not for the purpose of making the pain greater, as generally believed. Thus, in every way, the Brotherhood strives, not to increase the penitent's self-imposed suffering, but to mitigate it as mercifully as possible—within the bounds of what to them constitutes reasonable penance. Flagellation is the first form of penance; hence the incisions down the back constitute the initiation of a new member.

The historic background of the Penitent Brotherhood in New Mexico is very clearly indicated in the old Spanish chronicles and in official records of Church and State in the New Mexican Archives. From these it appears that the existing Brotherhood is a genuine survival of the Third Order of St. Francis, introduced into New Mexico at the time of the Conquest. As members of this Third Order, especially designed for the laity, many of the Spanish conquerors and leading settlers, both men and women, directed in their wills that they be buried "in the habit of our Father Saint Francis, of whose Third Order I am a member."

Also viewed in the light of this historic past, all effort may be discounted which seeks to trace the origin of the so-called "barbaric" practices of the *Penitentes* to contact with savage Indian tribes—ignoring the fact that these practices were prevalent in Europe long before the discovery of the New World! What the Pueblo Indians thought of these "barbaric" customs of the

Christians has already been quoted in the words of Fray Alonso de Benavides. But thirty-two years before the Benavides Memorial was published, an earlier record gives us reason to believe that the penances of the *Penitentes* today are no more severe than were those of the Franciscans who first instituted the rites in New Mexico.

On March 20, 1598, Don Juan de Oñate, with his soldiers, priests, and colonists, stopped on the bank of a small stream to observe Holy Week. A description of this occasion is furnished by Captain Gaspar Pérez de Villagrá in the Eleventh Canto of his epic poem, the *Historia de la Nueva Mexico*, published twelve years later in Spain:

"The army again broke camp and we journeyed onward until we reached the banks of another stream. The friars named this river the *Sacramento* for the reason that we arrived at its banks on Holy Thursday, the feast of the Blessed Sacrament. In order to observe properly this most holy day, Don Juan ordered a large chapel built. In the center we placed a representation of the Holy Sepulcher. A special guard of honor stood watch the entire day and night. Here in the evening the priests and all the officers and men came and devoutly, on their knees, with tears in their eyes, begged forgiveness for their sins. They prayed to Our Blessed

Lord, that He, who walked with safety upon the waters, He who led the children of Israel through the trackless deserts, would have mercy and compassion on them and lead them safely through the arid places through which they wandered. They asked Him to guard over them and aid them to carry His Holy Faith to the remote regions of New Mexico.

"The night was one of prayer and penance for all. The women and children came barefoot to pray at the holy shrine. The soldiers, with cruel scourges, beat their backs unmercifully until the camp ran crimson with their blood. The humble Franciscan friars, barefoot and clothed in cruel thorny girdles, devoutly chanted their doleful hymns, praying forgiveness for their sins.

"Don Juan, unknown to anyone except me, went to a secluded spot where he cruelly scourged himself, mingling bitter tears with the blood which flowed from his many wounds. This continued throughout the camp till early morn. . . . Geronimo and I took example from these worthy ones and underwent like punishment. What lessons we learned from what we observed that day!"

This early record is not, of course, the first instance of public penance in the New World. It must be borne in mind that New Mexico was a Province and an integral part of Old Mexico; and that the priests and colonists brought with them the customs then prevailing not only in Mexico, but in Spain itself. Can anyone believe that Villagrá did not include that passage as of pertinent interest, worthy of the complete approval of the Spanish monarch to whom it was addressed?

It is unnecessary to recall the fact that the custom of flagellation was then widespread throughout Europe, continuing in some parts of Spain even into the Nineteenth Century. As regards religious penance in Old Mexico, even so late a book as Mme. Calderon de la Barca's *Life in Mexico*, published in 1843, gives many instances of forms of penance similar to those witnessed in New Mexico today. In fact, none of those witnessed today may be said to have originated in New Mexico. Even the *Penitente Tinieblas* has its counterpart in a much more severe ceremony witnessed by Mme. de la Barca in a church in Mexico City. And none of the forms of penance in the New World differed from those of the Old. It is, therefore, apparent that the *Penitente* rituals stem directly from Christian sources, with no aboriginal admixture whatever.

Following the Sixteenth- and Seventeenth-Century references of Villagrá and Benavides, a later document records the re-establishment of the Third Order of St. Francis in New Mexico, soon after the Reconquest by

De Vargas in 1692, with chapels of the Third Order at Santa Cruz and Santa Fe. This document, *Information Given to Governor Chacon by the Reverend Father-Custodian Fray Cayetano José Bernal. 17 September 1794,* is also interesting as showing the various feasts and patronal Saints' Days especially celebrated by the Third Order:

"In each of the two mentioned Villas, Santa Cruz de la Cañada and Santa Fe, exists the Venerable Third Order of Penitence, founded from the beginning of the Re-Conquest of this province, under the licensed authority of the Prelates of our own Seraphic Religion, as the immediate and legitimate superiors of the same.

"The Venerable Third Order of our Holy Father St. Francis [was founded] almost from the beginning of the Re-Conquest, although no one knows the exact year, with prior license from the Prelates of our Seraphic Religion as its immediate and legitimate superiors, to whom alone pertain its knowledge and government, as stated in the many declarations and confirmatory Bulls of many Roman Pontiffs, by which it is classified as separate from the Brotherhoods, with which it has nothing in common, being a true Order, like the First which is professed by the Religious, although with distinct rules and constitution.

"These alone [of Santa Cruz and Santa Fe] existed,

and have existed, and now exist, thanks to the devotion of the brothers of the Third Order; and thus its fund is that which pays for, in La Cañada, the fiesta of San Luis, King of France, and that of the Immaculate Conception, as its patrons; and for singing a Mass one Sunday in each month, with procession. But always this is pledged, or it would be necessary for the minister to do it without recompense and out of pure devotion, since the alms-fund would not be sufficient, there being few members of the Third Order.

"That of the Villa of Santa Fe expends it alms in paying for the ceremony of San Luis, for Masses with processions on the Second Sunday of every month, and for the Sermon of the Three Falls on Holy Friday, paid for according to custom; and for buying the wax candles for these ceremonies; and although in this Holy Third Order there are enough brothers, always it is pledged, as may be seen."

For a hundred years, these two chapels of the Third Order were maintained at Santa Cruz and Santa Fe. But a later inventory of churches, made by Vicar-General Fernandez in 1826, mentions the chapel of the Third Order adjoining the parochial church in Santa Fe as being then "so lacking in everything required for the celebration of the Mass that orders were given for the discontinuation of its use for this purpose."

This would seem to indicate that certain changes had taken place in the status of the Third Order in New Mexico, which, indeed was the case. In 1828 the Mexican Government passed a law expelling all who were of Spanish birth from the country, unless they renounced Spain and became citizens of the Republic of Mexico. Many of the Spanish-born Franciscans, it is believed, had already left the country, soon after Mexican Independence; which perhaps explains the dismantled condition of the Chapel of the Third Order in Santa Fe in 1826. But the law of 1828 caused the general exodus of all who were not willing to renounce Spanish allegiance. From this time on, the Third Order in New Mexico ceased to have a canonical existence. It could only exist under the authority of the Franciscans, and this authority ceased when the Franciscans left New Mexico. Consequently, the remaining lay members of the Third Order were left without spiritual guidance or authority; but this did not deter them from continuing the customs inherited from the time of the Conquest.

Even before the departure of the Franciscans, many changes had occurred, which were of a nature to make the people of New Mexico self-concentrative and generally unamenable to the too far-distant control of Mexico. In a religious as well as a political sense, New

Mexico had long suffered from the centralization of government in Mexico. For military and political reasons, the once widely spread, flourishing missions had been contracted to a narrower radius. Most of the priests lived in the Spanish villages, away from the outlying missions, which they visited in rotation. A ruinous condition of many missions and parish churches is recorded in old documents, indicating a generally lax supervision of the clergy from the seat of the bishopric at Durango, in Mexico. A journey from Durango to the Northern Province took several months, going and coming. Santa Fe received an apostolic visit from Bishop Martin Elizacochea in 1737; and another from Bishop Pedro Tamaron in 1760. In 1810 Don Pedro Pino, sent as a delegate to the Spanish Cortez, complained that he, who was then fifty years old, had never in his life seen a Bishop or known how a Bishop looked or dressed, until he came to Spain! Within New Mexico, too, the distances were also great, and equally arduous—as they are today. Consequently, the people in the remote Spanish villages received possibly fewer visitations from the priests than did the Indian pueblos.

It is not, therefore, to be wondered at that the people of isolated northern New Mexico had—even before the departure of the Franciscans and probably not without their approval—come to rely largely upon themselves and their long-existing Brotherhoods for the performance of certain religious rites. Nor is it strange that they were loath to relinquish these functions after the advent in the middle Nineteenth Century of priests who were not of their own country and background, or Franciscans. Not until the arrival of Archbishop Lamy and the French priests in the 1850's was any objection raised to the forms of penance practiced by the members of the Penitent Brotherhood. Public penance had indeed been banned by Papal Bulls, from as early as 1349; but the edicts had not been entirely successful in suppressing the old customs even in Europe. In New Mexico, neither the Franciscans nor the few secular priests who succeeded them had—as far as any records show—opposed the traditional forms of voluntary self-inflicted penance.

Doubtless it was during the time of the departure of the Franciscans and the coming of the French priests, when there were only a few secular priests left for all the huge parishes in New Mexico, that the Penitent Brotherhood established its firm hold on the people. There were, of course, other lesser *Cofradías,* or Brotherhoods, in New Mexico, apart from the true Orders. These doubtless merged with what remained of the original Third Order of St. Francis, in the traditional observance of Lent and Holy Week, thereby increasing the strength of *Los Hermanos de Luz*. The *Penitente* services—apart from the flagellation—are based very largely upon those of the Church, and the Rules are in a general sense similar to those of the canonical Third Order of St. Francis.

Parts of the *Penitente* ritual have an ancestry of great age. This is particularly true of the *alabados*, or hymns, patiently written down in small, much thumbed copybooks or transmitted by memory. In verse forms, these *alabados* have the earmarks of Fifteenth- or Sixteenth-Century Spain. The music to which these hymns are sung is somewhat reminiscent of Gregorian chants, but often with a wilder, more primitive strain, particularly in the case of songs sung by an individual penitent, which suddenly startle the listener with the piercing note of the *saeta*, "arrow-song" of Seville—undoubtedly of Moorish origin. These shrill songs of religious fervor suddenly lifted above the bare desert have the effect of poising the single soul against space. The longer hymns, with an interminable number of verses, are sung in what purports to be unison, but with the unevenness of the march over rough ground, the interrupting thud of whips, and especially the high notes of the *pito* which has no harmonic relation to the pitch of the voices, the general effect is that of a curious harmonic dissonance. This peculiar quality of the music is so moving that, once having heard it, one willingly makes a pilgrimage any, or every, year to hear it again.

The words of the songs are very beautiful in the Spanish originals. Essentially mystic in spirit, they have a direct simplicity, an "earthy" concreteness of expression similar to that of our Seventeenth-Century metaphysical poets. One of the *alabados* in a small copybook in my possession is a funeral hymn sung as the body is being carried to the *Campo Santo*. It is the dead man who speaks and says good-by to the world he is leaving. The song is typically Spanish in its stoic acceptance of life and death, and in its mixture of the homely and the Divine. Other *alabados* are long narratives of the whole story of Christ's life and death; shorter ones in praise of the Virgin; and many, of course, apply directly to the discipline of penance as a means of salvation or purification of the heart.

N this account, emphasis has been placed perhaps unduly on the forms of penance practiced by the *Penitentes* as a curious survival of the Middle Ages; but not, I hope, to the exclusion of the sense of their underlying intensely religious spirit. This spirit is deeply rooted and closely interwoven in the texture of the lives of the Spanish people of New Mexico, and the Lenten ceremonies furnish the most native expression of that spirit. No springtime comes without one's being conscious that everywhere in the small villages, in the high mountain foothills, or along the Rio Grande Valley, groups of simple, sincere people are making their pilgrimages of expiation, through snow and sleet, or under budding fruit trees, to distant shrines, or to neighboring cross-topped hills. The enduring faith and the survival of the forms of that faith are alike remarkable.

We have seen how the Brotherhood came to forfeit its sanction by the Church; or, to be more exact, how the Church—through the long hard days of early settlement, the isolation of great distances, political conflict and change—lost its hold on the Brotherhood. The Brotherhood, however, did not lose its hold on the early precepts and practices of the Franciscans, which it still maintains, with the tenacity of an isolated, simple people to age-old customs and traditions. And, this in spite of all opposition, for the Church has from time to time prohibited the public penances of the *Penitentes*, under threat of excommunication. A wiser policy leaves the ultimate dissolution of such practices to time, which now, with the quickly accelerated modern pace, obliterates many old customs far more rapidly than opposition could. No Mass, of course, is ever said in the chapel of a *Penitente Morada*; but the members of the Brotherhood are all Catholics, and regularly attend Mass in the Church, and are not denied the Sacraments. The effort of the Church is gradually to reabsorb this truly religious zeal and direct it into more moderate forms of expression.

Today in all *Penitente* communities during Holy Week, the church doors stand open to receive those who come to pray or to make the regular Stations of the Cross. Sometimes a procession from the *Morada*, carrying an image of Christ, meets a procession of women from the church carrying an image of the Virgin Mary. In the courtyard of the church, the Virgin sorrowfully meets and kisses her Son. The tiny courtyard is crowded with men, women and children who recite prayers and sing an *alabado* which tells the story of this meeting. The entire community takes part in such dramatized observances of Holy Week. Women, not openly, but often privately, undergo severe forms of penance. As a milder form of penance, the women in Santa Fe, when they visited the churches on Holy Thursday, used to put grains of wheat in their shoes.

Flagellants and others actually performing penance do not as a rule enter the churches, from which they were excluded by order of Archbishop Salpointe, the successor of Archbishop Lamy. In connection with the threat of excommunication then made, one often hears it said that the black cowls worn by the *Penitentes* are for the purpose of escaping detection. This has no basis in fact, for the leading *Hermanos,* and all not actually performing penance, have their faces uncovered. The reason for the masks goes deeper. The head covering is traditional, derived from the penitent's desire to remain humble and unknown in his penance, with no idea of obtaining vainglory through its performance. Head-masks are still worn by the penitents in the Holy Week processions in Seville, and a painting by Goya, *Los Disciplinantes,* shows a procession in which all the penitents wear cowls, or the traditional cone-shaped hoods, of the various *Cofradías.*

Incidentally, this painting by Goya shows one form of cross-bearing which I have seen at only one village in New Mexico. The penitent, instead of dragging a long heavy cross, has the main beam of a shorter cross bound horizontally to the back of his outstretched arms. Every community differs somewhat from the others in its form of ritual and penance. In some villages, more pageantry is involved, recalling the Church processions witnessed in Taos by Gregg, and in Santa Fe by Davis, with their Pontius Pilates and Veronicas, Roman Centurions on foot or on horseback, and other trappings of religious dramatization. These impersonations are still annual features of Holy Week in Old Mexico and survive in some form or other in many New Mexican villages.

At Llano, near Taos, I once saw a small ceremony in the patio of a *Morada*, where Pilate and the Centurions were grouped about a recumbent Christ in the Sepulcher, small boys taking the parts of the Centurions, and a small girl the part of Veronica. An unusual musical feature was the combination of an Indian drum with the *pito*, an effect that would certainly have appealed to a modern composer. Also, in a tiny mountain village, I have seen a much gentler form of the *Tinieblas*, held not in the *Morada*, but in the very beautiful old adobe church, where the first prayer spoken was "for those who have evil intentions against us," and where the whole spirit was softened to a plea for merciful intercession.

Of late years, it has become quite the fashion for vis-

iting *Americanos* to go "sleuthing *Penitentes*" around Easter time, the favorite method being to drive up in a large high-powered car with headlights turned full upon any chance procession or on the very door of the *Morada*. Naturally, opposition is aroused; and lurid tales are told of threats made by the *Hermano Mayor*, who very conveniently for this purpose wears a shoulder holster under his coat. But if you are courteously inclined, a like courtesy will be extended—within the bounds of what you may or may not be permitted to see. For the ceremonies, although performed in the open plazas or countryside, are not for an audience, but for the participants. Your presence will be tolerated only if you remain respectfully deferential.

It was with a sense of deep obligation that we paid our call upon the *Hermano Mayor* at Abiquiu, on the Saturday morning of our departure. White-haired and gentle, he sat in the best room of his small adobe house to receive us; and we were reminded again by his finely drawn aristocratic features of the paintings of El Greco or Velasquez. We thought, too, of the fact that, although he could not wear the brown robe of a member of the Third Order of St. Francis, such as the grandees of the Re-Conquest directed in their wills that they be buried in, he was spiritually of their companionship.

We took a last look at the small plaza, completely

asleep like most of the inhabitants of the village, and turned our faces south and toward, on the next morning, Easter Day, quite another sort of New Mexican ceremony—the sun-worshiping spring Corn Dance of the Santo Domingo Indians.

NOTES

The following translations of alabados, *or* hymns, *are from a small* Penitente *copy-book, much worn from use. This book includes nineteen songs; one of these, recounting the whole story of Christ's life and Resurrection, has one hundred and forty stanzas.*

NUESTRO PADRE JESÚS

Por ser mi divina luz
¡Ay! Jesús de l'alma mia,
Llevando en mi compania
A nuestro Padre Jesús.

Escuchen bien, pecadores,
Los esclavos de Jesús,
Cumplan con el juramento
De nuestro Padre Jesús.

Escuchen bien, pecadores,
Alabanzas de Jesús,
Y contemplen esta luz
De nuestro Padre Jesús.

¡Oigan! me bien pecadores,
Y contemplen esta luz
Que es la divina corona
De nuestro Padre Jesús.

Aclamarán los cofrados
Aclamarán esta luz
Para llevar en su pecho
A nuestro Padre Jesús.

OUR FATHER JESUS

By this Divine Light,
O Jesus of my soul,
I take in my brotherhood
Our Father Jesus.

Listen well, sinners,
All ye slaves of Jesus,
And comply with your oath
To our Father Jesus.

Listen well, sinners,
To the glories of Jesus,
And contemplate this Light
Of our Father Jesus.

Listen well, sinners,
And contemplate this Light
Which is the Divine Crown
Of our Father Jesus.

Acclaiming these brothers,
Acclaiming this Light,
That you may take in your heart
Our Father Jesus.

Pecadores, pecadores,
Que padecen por Jesús,
Que venerán a los clavos
De nuestro Padre Jesús.

En los brazos estrechados
Aqui esta divina luz,
En su compania lleva
A nuestro Padre Jesús.

Los clavos que veneramos
 Aquí esta divina luz
En su compania lleva
A nuestro Padre Jesús.

Hermanos verdaderos
Que acompañan a Jesús
No quiebren el mistério
De nuestro Padre Jesús.

La dolorosa pasión
Que Jesús paso por voz,
Cumplan con el juramento
En agradecimiento á Dios.

Felices los que a Dios sirven
En su Sagrada pasión

Sinners, sinners,
Who suffer for Jesus
And who will feel the nails
Of our Father Jesus.

In these arms outstretched,
Here is the Divine Light!
In His brotherhood we take
Our Father Jesus.

The nails we shall suffer,
And this Divine Light,
And in His brotherhood take
Our Father Jesus.

Brothers who truly
Accompany Jesus,
Do not break the mystery
Of our Father Jesus.

This painful passion
Jesus suffered for you,
Comply with your oath
And be thankful to Jesus.

Happy those who serve God
In His Sacred Passion

Y que reciben en su pecho
En la Santa comunión.

Hermanos que con su luz
Van padeciendo por Dios
Allá estarán en su reino
Con nuestro Padre Jesús.

Los que creen en la iglesia
Y en esta divina luz
Son esclavos verdaderos
De nuestro Padre Jesús.

Vamos todos de rodias
Alabando aqui esta luz
Con un credo y un salve
A nuestro Padre Jesús.

Fin—Fin

And in their breasts receive Him
In the Holy Communion.

Brothers who in this Light
Are suffering for God,
You will be in His kingdom
With our Father Jesus.

Those who believe in this Church
And in this Divine Light
Are the slaves truly
Of our Father Jesus.

Let us all go on our knees,
Worshiping this Light,
With a *Credo* and a *Salve*
To our Father Jesus.

THE END

DIOS TOCA EN ESTA MISIÓN

Dios toca en esta misión
Las puertas de Su clemencia,
Penitencia, penitencia,
Si quieres tu salvación.

Penitencia, penitencia,
Ya no peques, hombre atros,
Examina tu conciencia,
Ven al templo oye la voz.

Tiempo es de hacer penitencia,
Hombre que estas divertido
Al no haber te arrepentido
Examina tu conciencia.

Llora ya con llanto tierno
No abiolentes la sentencia;
Antes de caer al infierno—
Penitencia, penitencia.

Mira aquí a Dios humanado
Dirigido aquí hace años
Diciendonos Dios rogado
Ya no peques, hombre atros.

GOD KNOCKS AT THIS MISSION

God knocks at this Mission
On the doors of His mercy,
Penitence, penitence,
If you wish salvation.

Penitence, penitence,
Sin no more, unfortunate man,
Examine your conscience,
Come to the temple and hear the Voice!

It is time to make penance,
You who have been too busy
To take warning to repent,
Examine your conscience!

Now weeping soft tears,
Do not avoid the sentence,
Before you fall into Hell,
Penitence, penitence.

Look here at your God become human!
Pleading from then until now,
God has been merciful, saying
Sin no more, unfortunate man!

Como nacío no advertia
Ya si pequé con violencia
Es buen tiempo todavía
Examina tu conciencia.

¡Llora, llora, penitente,
Llora tu culpa perdida
En lágrimas derretidas
Llora tu culpa insolente!

Haz un auto verdadero
Reconciliate con Dios
Hoy te dice un misionero
Ven al templo oye la voz.

¡Tu pierdes sin esperanza
Si sigues pecando atros!
No continues la venganza,
Ven al templo oye la voz.

Si en el mundo te entretienes,
El tiempo se va veloz,
Antes de que te condenes
Ven al templo oye la voz.

Ya se me acabó el aliento
Ya me voy al Redentor,

If from birth without heeding
You have sinned with violence,
There is still time, even yet—
Examine your conscience.

Weep, weep, *Penitente*,
Weep until sin is lost
In redeeming tears—
Weep for your insolent fault!

This is the time truly
To become reconciled with God,
Today the Missionary tells you,
Come to the temple and hear the Voice!

You are lost without hope
If you keep on sinning,
Don't call down the vengeance—
Come to the temple and hear the Voice!

If by the world absorbed,
The time goes swiftly—
Before you are condemned,
Come to the temple and hear the Voice!

Now that my strength is failing,
I go to the Redeemer!

Y si quieres reponerte
¡Ya no peques, hombre atros!

Ven a Mi te estrechare
En Mis brazos ambos dos,
¿Porque no llegas, porque?
¡Ven al templo oye la voz!

¡Alerto! que estas perdido,
Haz un examin veloz
Ya si mal entretenido
¡Ven al templo oye la voz!

Llega a la mesa Sagrada,
Deja la culpa feroz
Venid solteras, casadas
¡Ven al templo oye la voz!

¿Y entonces necio imagina
Que diras, ante de Dios?
Esta es mi Santa Doctrina
¡Ven al templo oye la voz!

¡Vuelva mi Dios Soberano!
Al evangelio de Dios
El pecador es hurtado
¡Ven al templo oye la voz!

Fin—Fin

Come, if you want to be pardoned,
Come to the temple and hear the Voice!

Come to My arms outstretched,
Both arms, to enfold you!
Why don't you come, why not?
Come to the temple and hear the Voice!

Make haste before you are lost!
Examine quickly to see
If your pastimes are evil—
Come to the temple and hear the Voice!

Come to the Sacred Hill,
Having stopped sinning,
Come, both married and single,
Come to the temple and hear the Voice!

What then, fool, do you imagine
You can find to say before God?
This is the Holy Doctrine,
Come to the temple and hear the Voice!

Return, my God-Sovereign!
In the Gospel of God
The sinner is exhorted,
Come to the temple and hear the Voice!

THE END

ADIOS AL MUNDO

*Adios acompañamiento
Que me estuvieron velando,
Se me llego la hora y tiempo
De que me vallan sacando.*

*Adios mis amados padres
Que conservádon mi vida,
Ya se lléga la hora y tiempo
Ya se llegó mi partida.*

*Adios mis amados hijos,
Adios mi esposa querida,
Adios acompañamiento
Me voy para la otra vida.*

*Adios todos mis parientes,
Adios mi dulce morada,
Adios acompañamiento
Que ya voy en la jornada.*

*Adios acompañamiento
Se llegó la hora próspera,
Acompañen a mi entierro
Que es mi casa verdadera.*

GOOD-BY TO THIS WORLD

Good-by, all this company,
Who have been here at my wake,
The hour and time have come
When you must take me out.

Good-by, my loving parents,
Who conserved my life,
The hour and the time have come
For me to take my parting.

Good-by, my dear children,
And my wife, much beloved,
Good-by, all this company,
Now I go to the other life.

Good-by, all my kindred,
Good-by, my sweet *morada*,
Good-by, all my companions,
Now I go on the Journey.

Good-by, all this company,
My last hour has arrived;
Accompany me to my interment,
Which is my true house.

¡A! que penosa jornada,
Que camino tan atros!
Me voy para la otra vida
Lo determina mi Dios.

Ya se me acabó el aliento,
Ya se me acabó el sentido,
Dejo todas las delicias
De este mundo tan entretenido.

Acompañen me al sepulcro
Ya mi alma esta separada,
Ya va a comulgar sus penas,
De angeles acompañada.

Adios acompañamiento,
Que ya voy al Campo Santo,
Y toditos mis parientes
Gimen en amargo llanto.

Ya me separo de todos,
Y del mundo en general,
Hasta al vernos en la gloria
Y en el juicio universal.

Es posible Dios del alma
Que me a de llegar a ver

What a wearisome journey,
And such a hard road!
Now I am going to another life,
As my God has determined.

My strength has all left me,
And my mind has left me;
Now I leave all the pleasures
Of this world so confusing.

Accompany me to the sepulcher;
From me my soul has separated
And is going to confess its sins,
Surrounded by angels.

Good-by, all this company,
I am going to the Campo Santo,
And with me all my kindred,
Who weep bitter tears.

Now I separate from all,
And from the world in general,
Until we meet in glory
In the universal justice.

It is possible the God of my soul
May look in on me

Dentro de una sepultura
Donde mi cama a de ser.

La sepultura es mi cama,
La tierra mi propio centro;
Se atemorizan las almas
Al considerarse adentro.

Ya se va para la iglesia
Procidiendo en la oración,
Ya toditos mis parientes
Se les parte el corazón.

Que corazón no vera
Pensando en conciderar
Que este paso tan amargo
Todos lo tienen que dar!

Esta vida es un engaño,
Y nos tiene con desvelo,
Y los eres invertidos
Para sustentar el duelo.

De la tierra fui formado,
La tierra me a de comer;
La tierra me a sustantado,
Y al fin yo tierra ha de ser.

Inside the sepulcher
Where my bed will be.

The sepulcher is my bed,
The earth my proper seat;
And souls are frightened
When they consider themselves inside.

Now I am going to the church
Preceded by prayer,
And by all my kindred
Whose hearts are broken.

What one cannot see,
When he stops to consider,
That this bitter step,
All have got to take it!

This life is a riddle,
And it keeps us in a dream,
And we invent amusements
In order to support the pain.

From the earth I was made,
And the earth shall eat me,
The earth has sustained me,
And at last earth I shall be also.

Dios me crio con su poder
Y su Espiritu Divino,
Espero de su bondad
Me guie por buen camino.

Adios acompañamiento,
Pues ya todo esta cumplido;
Ponganmen en la sepultura
En la tierra del olvido.

De la nada fui formado
Por obra de mi criador,
Y en el juicio universal
El será mi defendor.

A Dios me póstro humillado
De mi culpa arrepentido,
El que me a de perdonar
Por lo mal que le a servido.

En Dios espero repóso,
En Dios espero consuelo,
De que en el juicio tremendo
Me ábra las puertas del cielo.

Soy de mi Jesús cofrado,
Soy de Jesús y sere,

God made me by the power
Of His Divine Spirit;
And I trust in His Goodness
He will guide me by a good road.

Good-by, all this company,
All has been completed;
Put me in the sepulcher
In the earth of forgetfulness.

Of nothing I was formed,
By the hands of the Creator,
And in the universal justice
He will be my defender.

To God I kneel humbly,
Of my faults repented;
He will forgive me
For the wrong way I have served Him.

In God I await to repose,
In God I await consolation,
Trusting in His tremendous justice
He will open Heaven's gate.

I am of my Jesus the brother,
I belong to Jesus and always will,

Porque con mi voluntad
A Jesús yo me entregaré.

Adios por ultima vez
Que me ven sobre la tierra,
Me echan a la sepultura
Que es la casa verdadera.

Adios todos los presentes
Que me van a acompañar,
Rezen algun sudario
Para poder alcanzar.

Adios todos mis proximos,
Toditos en general,
Encomienden mi alma a Dios,
No me vayan a olvidar.

Fin—Fin—Amén

Because I yielded gladly,
And to Jesus I surrender.

Good-by for the last time,
Those who see me on this earth,
Place me in the sepulcher
Which is truly my house.

Good-by, all those present,
All who accompany me,
Pray a *sudario*
In order to overtake me.

Good-by, all my neighbors,
All, all in general,
Commend my soul to God,
And do not forget me.

THE END—AMEN

The Order of St. Francis of Assisi was founded in 1210 by St. Francis of Assisi (Francis Bernadone), who died in 1226 and was canonized in 1228. The Second Franciscan Order of Poor Ladies (Poor Clares) was founded in 1212, through an appeal to St. Francis by his disciple, Clare of Assisi. In 1218 the Order of the Brothers and Sisters of Penance, now known as the Third Order of St. Francis, was established for the laity, who, without leaving the world for the cloister, might take the modified vows of this Order.

The Penitent Brotherhood, as it exists today in New Mexico, is hardly a separate religious sect, since it represents no radical departure from the parent stem; it may rather be called a "folk-survival," perpetuating formerly prevalent and authorized religious customs.

Apparently the first Protestant to recognize the origin of the Brotherhood as other than barbarian was Charles F. Lummis who in a chapter in his book, *The Land of Poco Tiempo,* correctly traced the ancestry of the Brotherhood to its Old World sources.

A later record of *Penitente* ceremonies and the present organization of the Brotherhood is found in a thesis on *Los Hermanos Penitentes,* by Mr. Laurence F. Lee, presented to the University of New Mexico in 1910. In this paper Mr. Lee quotes the following ceremonial

form of initiation which occurs on the eve of Ash Wednesday:

"As each *Penitente* knocks at the door of the *Morada*, he chants in Spanish a series of questions and receives chanted answers from within, the whole constituting an anthem of about six lines.

"*The Penitente*—God knocks at this Mission's door for His clemency.

"*The Hermanos de Luz*—Penance, penance, which seeks salvation.

"*The Penitente*—St. Peter will open to me the gate, bathing me with the light in the name of Mary, with the seal of Jesus. I ask this confraternity: Who gives this house of light?

"*The Hermanos de Luz*—Jesus.

"*The Penitente*—Who fills it with joy?

"*The Hermanos de Luz*—Mary.

"*The Penitente*—Who preserves it with faith?

"*The Hermanos de Luz*—Joseph.

"The devotee then enters and receives 'the thing of obligation,' the first step in the penance done during Holy Week. This is the seal which is administered by the *Sangrador* and consists of three gashes down and three across the back. It is said that the *Sangrador* must be quite skilled in performing this duty, as he uses a crude instrument, a piece of broken glass or flint, and must cut just deep enough to miss the muscles of the back.

"The penitent then usually asks: 'For the love of God, the Three Meditations of the Passion of Our Lord!'

"The answer to this request is in the form of six strokes from a rawhide lash, three on one side and three on the other side of the spine. The *Sangrador* firmly believes that the more zealous he is in performing his duty, the greater is his reward in the next world.

"The *Hermano's* zeal increases with his punishment and he next demands the Five Wounds of Christ: the Seven Last Words, the Forty Days in the Wilderness, each demand being prefaced by the formula 'for the love of God.'

"The answer to each demand is an increased number of strokes. It is seldom that the extreme number of strokes is reached, however, as the flagellant faints before it is nearly completed. He is then taken to the *Coadjutor*, who bathes his wounds in a strong tea made of 'Romero Weed.'"

It is interesting to note that the first question and response of this ceremony are identical with the opening words of the hymn *Dios Toca en Este Misión*, translated above; and that the following questions and answers may be found in stanzas quoted by Mme. Calderón de la Barca in her *Life in Mexico*.

> *¿Quién a esta casa da luz?*
> *Jesús.*
> *¿Quién la llena de alegría?*
> *María.*
> *¿Y quién la abraza en la fé?*
> *José.*

> *Luego bien claro se vé*
> *Que siempre habra contricion,*
> *Teniendo en el corazón*
> *A Jesús, María, y José.*

> Who gives light to this house?
> Jesus.
> Who fills it with joy?
> Mary.
> Who kindles faith in it?
> Joseph.

> Thus it is clearly seen
> That always having contrition,
> We keep in our hearts
> Jesus, Mary, and Joseph.

Mme. Barca says that she found this printed poem pinned on all the doors of a house in Mexico where she was staying; with the following instructions printed beneath the poem: "The most illustrious Bishop of Monte-Rey, Don Fray de Jesús María Balaunzaran, hereby ordains and grants, along with the Bishops of Puebla, Durango, Valladolid, and Guadalajara, two hundred days of indulgence to all those who devoutly repeat the above ejaculation, and invoke the sweet names of Jesus, Mary, and Joseph."

The first part of this poem is also quoted by Alex M. Darley in his *Passionists of the Southwest,* published in 1893. It is interesting to see how the supposedly lurid *Penitente* ceremonies incorporate prayers and verses originally of Church origin! Darley was apparently a free-lance Protestant missionary in Colorado, and his book is as inaccurate and sensational as were most early Protestant accounts of the *Penitentes.*

Mr. Lee's thesis is one of the first accurate accounts of the *Penitentes,* and the present organization of the Brotherhood. The organization, however, varies slightly in the different communities. According to Mr. Lee the officers include: *The Hermano Mayor* (Older Brother); *Celador* (Warden); *Coadjutor* (Helper); *Infermero* (Nurse); *Mandatario* (Collector); *Maestro de Novicios* (Teacher of Novices); *Secretario* (Secretary); *Sangrador* (Pricker), the officer who inflicts the seal of the *Penitentes* upon the backs of the members; *Rezador*

(One who prays); *Pitero* (Fluter). The officers taken as a body are called the *Hermanos de Luz* (Brothers of Light).

Occasionally the office of *Hermano Mayor* is hereditary, from father to son; but in most communities he, like all the other officers, is elected annually.

Practically every *Penitente Morada* features a *Carreta del Muerto* in its Holy Week processions. Some of the images are crude; others very meticulously carved. The figure of Death sheltered in a chapel adjoining the church at Trampas is remarkable in that the shoulders, stomach-muscles, and hips are beautifully carved in semblance of the living flesh, but with the ribs carved *outside* the chest; and the whole painted white. The hips end in a square block to which the movable legs are fastened with wooden pegs; and the head, above the accurate realism of the body, is a very much simplified death-mask, with inset mother-of-pearl eyes.

Chimayo was said to excel in the production of extremely realistic images, which its wood-carvers supplied to other villages. Many of these found their way into the churches, but the Nineteenth-Century French priests objected to the deeply ensanguined realism of their Crucifixions, Saints, and Martyrs and put a stop to their production—as far as the Church was concerned. As mentioned in the text, this realism came direct from Spain; the sculptor, Montañes, a contemporary of Velasquez, excelled in it.

The *Penitente Morada* was probably in the beginning only a single cell. Examples, or ruins, of this older form may still be seen in the hills, half-sunk in the ground. This one-room unit was followed by the usual present form, including the secret room of the members and an adjoining chapel which is open to all at certain times. There is nothing more mysterious about the inner room of the *Morada* than there is about the membership "lodge" of any secret society. In it are kept the whips, chains, food, and clothing of the members, as well as the large crosses and the *Carreta del Muerto* when not in use. As a matter of fact, there is nothing at all mysterious about the *Penitentes,* except that many of the processions occur at night, and are supposed to be secret. But they were never secret until the *"Anglos"* came, and after the French priests attempted their suppression. Before that, they were of the order of the day, witnessed or participated in by all. The thrill of supposedly mysterious nocturnal rites was added by the imaginative *"Anglos."* The present secrecy is occasioned in part by the not unnatural desire of the members to perform their rites of penance in a deserved privacy.

The heavy crosses dragged by the *Penitentes* are made

of pine, the main timber about seventeen feet in length, and the weight of a cross averages about two hundred and fifty pounds. The *disciplinas,* or whips, are sometimes made of heavily braided and knotted cords, but more usually now of leaves stripped from the yucca plant. The whips are immersed in salt water, making them pliable. The salt may, somewhat unappreciably, increase the sting—but it has an antiseptic value also. The Romero Weed, in a solution of which the *Penitente's* back is bathed, is Rosemary.

The more one delves into the historic background, the more certain one becomes that there is nothing in *Penitente* ceremonies traceable to any forms or practices extraneous to those of the Church. Here, in a scene witnessed by Mme. Calderón de la Barca in the church of San Agustine in Mexico City, in 1843, is what may be taken as a forerunner of the *Tinieblas* in a *Penitente Morada:*

"The scene was curious. About one hundred and fifty men, enveloped in cloaks and serapes, their faces entirely concealed, were assembled in the body of the church. A monk had just mounted the pulpit, and the church was dimly lighted, except where he stood in bold relief, with his gray robes and cowl thrown back, giving a full view of his high bald forehead and expressive face. His discourse was a rude but very forcible and eloquent description of the torments prepared in hell for impenitent sinners. The effect of the whole was very solemn. It appeared like a preparation for the execution of a multitude of condemned criminals. When the discourse was finished, they all joined in prayer with much fervor and enthusiasm, beating their breasts and falling upon their faces. Then the monk stood up, and in a very distinct voice, read several passages of Scripture descriptive of the sufferings of Christ. The organ then struck up the *Miserere,* and all of a sudden the church was plunged in profound darkness; all but a sculptured representation of the Crucifixion, which seemed to hang in the air illuminated. I felt rather frightened, and would have been very glad to leave the church, but it would have been impossible in the darkness. Suddenly a terrible voice in the dark cried, 'My brothers! When Christ was fastened to the pillar by the Jews, He was *scourged!*' At these words, the bright figure disappeared, and the darkness became total. Suddenly, we heard the sound of hundreds of scourges descending upon the bare flesh. I cannot conceive anything more horrible. Before ten minutes had passed, the sound became *splashing,* from the blood that was flowing.

"I have heard of these penitences in Italian churches,

and also that half of those who go there do not really scourge themselves; but here where there is such perfect concealment, there seems no motive for deception. Incredible as it may seem, this awful penance continued, without intermission, for half an hour! If they scourged *each other*, their energy might be less astonishing. We could not leave the church, but it was perfectly sickening; and had I not been able to take hold of the Señora ——'s hand, and feel something human beside me, I could have fancied myself transported into a congregation of evil spirits. Now and then, but very seldom, a suppressed groan was heard, and occasionally the voice of the monk encouraging them by ejaculations, or by short passages from Scripture. Sometimes the organ struck up, and the poor wretches, in a faint voice, tried to join in the *Miserere*. The sound of the scourging is indescribable. At the end of half an hour, a little bell was rung, and the voice of the monk was heard, calling upon them to desist; but such was their enthusiasm, that the horrible lashing continued louder and fiercer than ever. In vain he entreated them not to kill themselves; and assured them that Heaven would be satisfied, and that human nature could not endure beyond a certain point. No answer, but the loud sound of the scourges, which are many of them iron, with sharp points that enter the flesh. At length, as if they were perfectly exhausted, the sound grew fainter, and little by little ceased altogether. We then got up in the dark, and with great difficulty, groped our way in the pitch darkness through the galleries and down the stairs, till we reached the door and had the pleasure of feeling the fresh air again. They say that the church floor is frequently covered with blood after one of these penances, and that a man died the other day in consequence of his wounds."

This quotation again makes one sure that the religious zeal of the Penitentes is not an innovation of the aboriginal soil of New Mexico!

Countless passages could be quoted regarding the custom of religious flagellation in the Old World, not confined to the Franciscans, but prevalent in other Orders and sects, and attaining such proportions in time of wars, famines and pestilence as to occasion Papal Bulls prohibiting the practice. One brief quotation, from *Belgium*, by Hugh Stokes, gives an idea of the general participation of the upper classes in this form of religious penance, as witnessed by a French visitor during the reign of Philip II:

"Nothing was more curious than the aspect of Brussels on the night of Holy Thursday. The streets and the public squares, as light as day in the flare of the torches, were crowded by penitents of the nobler classes. These gentlemen walked from church to church to kneel before the Stations and to weep over Christ's Tomb. Many of them, covered by a rough cloak, carried a heavy cross on their shoulders. Others, half clothed, flagellated their body, or whipped themselves with chains. Mingling the profane with the sacred, they displayed their wounds to the ladies who flocked to admire their divine ardor."

In New Mexico, but one source existed for the introduction of these Old World customs—that of the Third Order of St. Francis.

The Penitentes today are by no means confined, as sometimes stated, to the Rio Arriba, or upper Rio Grande valley. Although perhaps most numerous in this longest settled and still largely Spanish region, *Penitente Moradas* may be found far south along the Rio Grande, west beyond Mt. Taylor, east of the Sangre de Cristo range, and as far north as southern Colorado. For over two hundred years, the old province of New Mexico was under the exclusive custodianship of the Franciscan missionaries, and lay membership in the Third Order was as wide-spread as the Missions. Today the Penitent Brotherhood covers the same general territory as the old Missions. Nor was its origin "plebeian." Although its members naturally embraced all classes of society, the officers were the leading citizens and "great swells" of the Re-Conquest.

Bradford L. Prince in a chapter on the *Penitentes* in his *Spanish Mission Churches of New Mexico* says that for two centuries nearly every leading citizen was a member of the Third Order, as indicated in the old wills, which included a proviso to the following effect: "I direct that when God, our Lord, shall see fit to call me out of this present life, my body be enshrouded in the habit of our father, San Francisco, of whose Third Order I am a Brother, and that my funeral be modest [humilde]."

REFERENCES TO PENITENTES
(Chronological)

Gaspar Pérez de Villagrá, *Historia de la Nueva Mexico*. Alcala, Spain, 1610. Translated by Gilberta Espinosa, 1933.

Memorial of Fray Alonso de Benavides, 1630. Translated by Mrs. Edward E. Ayer, 1916.

Information Given to Governor Fernando Chacon, by the Reverend Father-Custodian, F. Cayetano José Bernal, 17 September, 1794. Church document, quoted in Salpointe, p. 159.

Report of Vicar-General Don Augustin Fernandez, of pastoral visitation of the Missions of New Mexico, 1826. Document, quoted in Salpointe, p. 159.

Josiah Gregg, *Commerce of the Prairies*, 1840. Vol. I, p. 47.

Mme. Calderón de la Barca, *Life in Mexico*. 1843.

W. W. H. Davis, *El Gringo*. 1856. Chapter XV.

Charles F. Lummis, *The Land of Poco Tiempo*. 1893.

Alex M. Darley, *The Passionists of the Southwest*. Pueblo, Colorado. 1893.

John G. Bourke, "Notes on the Language and Folk-Usage of the Rio Grande Valley." *Journal of American Folk-Lore*, April-June, 1896.

D. J. Flinn, "Penitentes in Taos." *Harper's Weekly*, about 1896.

Archbishop J. B. Salpointe, *Soldiers of the Cross; Notes on the Ecclesiastical History of New Mexico, Arizona, and Colorado*. 1898.

Laurence F. Lee, *Los Hermanos Penitentes*. Thesis, University of New Mexico, 1910. Printed in El Palacio, Santa Fe, January 31, 1920.

L. Bradford Prince, *Spanish Mission Churches of New Mexico.* 1916.

Aurelio M. Espinosa, "Los Hermanos Penitentes." *Catholic Encyclopedia.* Vol. XI, p. 635.

F. W. Hodge, "Note on Penitentes." *Memorial of Benavides,* p. 211.

H. H. Bancroft, *History of New Mexico and Arizona.*

R. E. Twitchell, *Leading Facts of New Mexican History; Old Santa Fe; New Mexican Archives.*

The above is source material. Modern writers who have recorded impressions of the *Penitentes,* in articles, plays, or stories include Mary Austin, Margaret Larkin, Elizabeth Shepley Sergeant, Harvey Fergusson, Raymond Otis, and Ruth Laughlin Barker.

www.ingramcontent.com/pod-product-compliance
Lightning Source LLC
Chambersburg PA
CBHW020052170426
43199CB00009B/258